HACKING ASSESSMENT

HACKING ASSESSMENT

10 Ways to Go Gradeless in a Traditional Grades School

Starr Sackstein

PUBLICATIONS

Hacking Assessment

© 2015 by Times 10 Publications

All rights are reserved. No part of this publication may be reproduced in any form or by any electronic or mechanical means, including information storage and retrieval systems, without permission in writing by the publisher, except by a reviewer who may quote brief passages in a review. For information regarding permission, contact the publisher at mark@times10books.com.

These books are available at special discounts when purchased in quantity for use as premiums, promotions, fundraising, and educational use. For inquiries and details, contact us: mark@times10books.com.

Published by Times 10 Publications

Cleveland, OH

http://hacklearningseries.com

Cover Design by Tracey Henterly

Interior Design by Steven Plummer

Editing by Ruth Arseneault

Library of Congress Control Number: 2015951075

ISBN: 978-0-9861049-1-6

First Printing: December, 2015

CONTENTS

ACKNOWLEDGEMENTS

N**O BOOK COULD** be written without the help of others, and this one is no exception. Thank you to Mark Barnes, who wanted me to share these ideas with other folks who are ready for this change in education.

I'd also like to acknowledge and thank the people who willingly provided anecdotes for the "Hack in Action" sections. Your stories enrich and add validity to this book; I'm hoping that, together, we will make meaningful change. Without Sarah Donovan, Garnet Hillman, Aric Foster (additionally for your support in the editing process), Adam Jones, Joy Kirr, Jimmy Bailey, and Jim Cordery, the book would have been flat, and only about my story.

A special thanks to Dr. Michael Curran who repeatedly answers my bat signal at a moment's notice and works hard to give me the best advice he has to offer. I'm grateful for our friendship.

Thank you to the students of World Journalism Preparatory School (WJPS), who patiently learned with me while I took this risk for the first time. Your candor and open-mindedness, as well as your challenges, made me a better teacher. A special thanks to Samantha Aversano and Anastasia Papatheodorou for allowing me to share your excellent work with the world.

Thank you to the administration of WJPS, who supported me while I took this risk and encouraged more teachers to get on board. I truly couldn't have done it without you.

To all of the dreamers and visionaries who know there's a better way that has yet to be found.

ABOUT THE *HACK* LEARNING SERIES

Hackers don't take realities of the world for granted;
they seek to break and rebuild what they don't like.
— Sarah Lacy, Author/Journalist

A HACKER IS SOMEONE who explores programmable systems and molds them into something different, often something better. Hackers are known as computer geeks—people who like to take applications and systems to places their designers never intended. Today, hackers are much more. They are people who explore many things both in and out of the technology world. They are tinkerers and fixers. They see solutions to problems that other people do not see. Steve Jobs and Mark Zuckerberg might be considered technology's greatest hackers. No one taught them how to build an operating system or a social network, but they saw possibilities that others couldn't see.

The *Hack Learning Series* is a collection of books written by people who, like Jobs and Zuckerberg, see things through a different lens. They are teachers, researchers, and consultants; they are administrators, professors, and specialists. They live to solve problems whose solutions, in many cases, already exist but may need to be hacked. In other words, the problem needs to be turned upside down or viewed from another perspective. Its fix may appear unreasonable to those plagued by the issue. To the hacker, though, the solution is evident, and with a little hacking it will be as clear and beautiful as a gracefully-designed smartphone or a powerful social network.

So many facets of learning need to be hacked: the Common Core, digital literacy, reluctant learners, special education, cultural diversity, teacher preparation, and school leadership, to name a few. When teachers, parents, administrators, and policymakers see the amazing insights that hackers can bring to various issues, they are sure to want more. Enter the *Hack Learning Series*—an evolving collection of books solving problems that impede learning in the world of education and beyond.

INSIDE THE BOOKS

Hack Learning books are written by passionate people who are experts in their fields. Unlike your typical education text, *Hack Learning* books are light on research and statistics and heavy on practical advice from people who have actually experienced the problems about which they write. Each book in the series contains chapters, called Hacks, which are composed of these sections:

- **The Problem:** Something educators are currently wrestling with that doesn't yet have a clear-cut solution

- **The Hack:** A brief description of the prescribed solution

- **What You Can Do Tomorrow:** Ways you can take the basic hack and implement it right away in bare-bones form

- **A Blueprint for Full Implementation:** A step-by-step system for building long-term capacity

- **Overcoming Pushback:** A list of possible objections you might come up against in your attempt to implement this hack and how to overcome them

- **The Hack in Action:** A snapshot of an educator or group of educators who have used this hack in their work and how they did it

EDITOR'S PROMISE

I am so proud to be a contributing author and the editor of the *Hack Learning Series*, written by experts who are dedicated to improving teaching and learning. I promise that every *Hack Learning* book will provide powerful information, imagination, engaging prose, practical advice, and maybe even a little humor. When you read a *Hack Learning Series* book, you'll have solutions you didn't have before.

MARK BARNES, AUTHOR/SPEAKER/HACKER

INTRODUCTION

Goodbye, grades; hello, growth

FRUSTRATION. EVERY TIME I had to complete report cards I felt frustration bordering on anger. How was I supposed to communicate learning with one grade without making every student's learning seem the same? Averaged scores say very little about actual learning: any number of students can earn a B for many different combinations of reasons. A gifted student who does little work may receive the same grade as a struggling student who has improved steadily throughout the course or a student who started off strongly but performed poorly in the last quarter. Unfortunately, in high school a single number or letter grade on a report card is supposed to communicate a great deal of important information.

Every time a grading period ended, I struggled with how to assess my students meaningfully and became increasingly less satisfied with how the system expected me to do it. Something had to change—I was doing my students a disservice even if they didn't realize it.

Assessment must be a conversation, a narrative that enhances students' understanding of what they know, what they can do, and what needs further work. Perhaps even more important, they need to understand how to make improvements and how to recognize when legitimate growth has occurred.

Two years ago I started dabbling with the process of eliminating grades, initially taking the risk in one of my elective classes. It was a safe testing ground to pilot the idea, as the class wasn't essential for graduation. After getting mostly positive feedback from students despite my relatively novice understanding of the practice, it was time to go all-in. I decided to make the move at the beginning of the school year, accepting that it would likely be messy and that many things would need to change as we went forward. With the permission of my administration, I sent a letter home to parents, and when students arrived we immediately started talking about learning.

As a high school English teacher in a small New York City school, I work in a program that is somewhat unconventional, comprised of five different classes of varying content and student grade levels. The year I began to experiment with the no-grades classroom, my program was as follows: Ninth grade ICT Journalism (an inclusion class, which in this instance operated without the support of a special education teacher), 11th grade Newspaper with students of varying skill levels, 12th grade Newspaper, AP Literature and Composition, and Publications Finance (taught alongside two math teachers who were new to the subject), for a grand total of 152 students. Undaunted by this huge undertaking, I hoped my enthusiasm and purpose would engage the students in a meaningful dialogue.

As with any new endeavor, running a no-grades classroom came with some challenges. Although I'd taught all of the classes before, I hadn't done so without grades, and time management became an issue. At times, the shift away from traditional grades was exceptionally challenging: it was much easier, I realized, to "just" put a grade on student work.

However, the immediate impact of the new system on my students encouraged me to persevere through these difficulties. My lower-level learners were enticed by the idea of a no-grades classroom, often asking why other teachers weren't taking the same approach. They liked the idea of not being judged; they hadn't had success in a traditional space, often being negatively labeled because learning was more challenging for them.

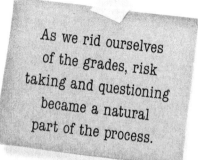

As we rid ourselves of the grades, risk taking and questioning became a natural part of the process.

Most of our learning and practice happened in class, so I was able to support students as they worked. Whereas almost none of them had been empowered to be an "expert" before, they developed expertise in different areas, such as identifying active headlines, writing engaging leads, organizing effective articles, and attributing quotations properly. They appreciated being treated like capable students rather than having the teacher assume they would always back away from a challenge.

Since all students work at different paces, there would be no assigned additional nightly homework. Students were allowed to continue working on projects as they saw fit in and out of school, but there was no reason to burden them with busy-work at home. Admittedly, this was a challenge at first. I had always given homework because I believed making students responsible for managing time and taking control of their own learning was a mark of rigorous pedagogy.

After teaching for many more years and not seeing positive results with some of my older practices, I researched and read widely and determined that much of what I thought was good practice really wasn't. While I no longer believed that giving homework is good practice, I had to remind myself that my students were getting an education that was often more rigorous than before, even without the homework. Rigor doesn't necessarily have to do with the amount of work assigned, but rather the difficulty and intensity of the problem or project.

Throughout this book, you will encounter many of the challenges I faced while successfully making changes. After working within a traditional system for more than a decade, there is a deprogramming process that still occasionally causes me to pause. However, after seeing increased student commitment to learning once grades were eliminated, I'm constantly reminded of what truly motivates students: challenge, interest, and expectations, rather than a teacher's rules.

These changes were ideal in the journalism class. As we rid ourselves of the grades, risk taking and questioning became a natural part of the process. Students sought new programs online to test their ideas and the outcomes were amazing. For example, when it was time to create journalism ethics PSAs, students found different storyboarding apps and cartoon apps rather than choosing to film themselves, which was uncomfortable for quieter students. Each group developed a different twist on its assignment, which enriched the learning. The work was sound and creative, and learning was a positive experience for the students and for me.

My highest-level students weren't as excited by the idea; after all, most of the 12th grade advanced placement class defined themselves as "A" students and if I took this away from them, how would they know they were excelling? Achieving high grades is extremely important to an honor student. As a former honor student, I could empathize with their need for grades: I used to fight vigorously for every point I could get, just as they do. Looking back, the grade had little to do with the learning and more to do with my need to feel smart. Those high grades were like a bulletin to the world announcing my achievement. I can't imagine how much more I would have learned if I didn't feel the need to compete for better grades and instead had just focused on learning. Hard conversations had to happen. Tough questions had to be answered.

"What is achievement?"

The question lingered in the air. I gave the students time to record their thoughts and then they shared them in small groups. To many, achievement meant high grades in every class. This idea had to be challenged.

"What does getting an A really mean?"

We broke it down. Our debate opened with strong feelings and stronger opinions. By the end of the first discussion, I could tell that they appreciated this new idea, but many weren't willing to abandon their beloved grades.

Buy-in was most difficult for the juniors. Seeing that this was a critical year for college, most of them didn't like the idea of dealing with something new at this point in their educational careers. I couldn't blame them for their skepticism, but I assured them that it would all be okay. We continued to converse throughout the early days of the school year.

I had planned to speak with parents about the shift away from grades on open school night. Unfortunately, few parents attended; I had to reach them another way. Despite my discomfort with video, I started a YouTube channel so I could communicate progress and make learning transparent for parents and students. I committed to making a video a week, tracking both successes and challenges in our work. This channel ended up being a resource for my colleagues who were frustrated with grades. Unfortunately, few parents actually watched the videos.

Undeterred by these initial failed attempts to get parents on board, I received the feedback I needed by sending surveys home with the students. The most vocal parents shared their concerns, which were echoed by my high achievers and colleagues (and even by me at times), but instead of giving up I continued to push forward, focusing on the improvement students showed in their portfolios of work. The progress was undeniable. I then used the YouTube videos to display what I clearly saw in the work and the students saw it too.

I felt confident I was on the right track when I began to get feedback from colleagues around the world. As it turns out, many educators are frustrated with the current grading system and they, too, work in traditional schools. They articulated many of the same worries I'd been trying to address. How could I sustain a bold risk like this in an institution where no one else was doing it? How could a no-grades classroom succeed when I was still required to provide progress report grades and end-of-semester grades? The answer was to just keep going.

As the first progress report came due, it was time for self-assessment conferences. I met with every child to discuss his or her progress. Now, this wasn't the first time formal conversations had happened. Students had been receiving feedback from me and their peers the whole time, but this was the first time we had associated their progress with mastery of standards and equated progress to a traditional grade.

Although I was committed to eliminating grades, the school required me to maintain a standards-based online grade book that tracked each skill on a mastery scale and calculated a decaying average (a decaying average values the most recent iteration of the learning, rendering earlier versions as practice). Although maintaining an online grade book and traditional reporting was restrictive and upsetting—I even had several conversations with my principal about offering an alternative report for my students instead of the traditional progress report or report card—the school couldn't run its reports with any teacher's information missing, so I had to conform. This made me—and the students—very unhappy.

Since using an alternative grading system was non-negotiable, I chose to confer with each student and determine grades together.

These conversations were invaluable. As preparation, students filled out Google Forms about their finished work and the learning that was evidenced in it. We talked about what it means to truly master a skill. We looked at each student's body of work together and then we determined a preliminary grade to put on the progress report. Students had no surprises on report card day because they had selected their grades with me. I had no anxiety about students coming to me crying over the grade I had given them. Instead, everyone fully understood his or her level of achievement and had a plan for moving forward into the second half of the semester.

Was this perfect? No, but it was better for the moment. I had to accept less than perfect as "good enough" for the time being because of the school's requirements. My system didn't solve all of the issues with grading, but it was a step in the right direction. I suspect you could adapt a no-grades system for your working conditions as well.

The whole year went on like this. Projects included multiple opportunities for growth and feedback from peers and from me. Students raised questions about their learning and the classroom steadily became more student-centered. Students made decisions about their learning and their goals, and I provided strategies to achieve them, rather than assigning grades to a curriculum I had planned without their input. Reflection became a hallmark in the learning, a way for students to direct my reading of their work. In their reflections they told me what they were working on and asked for specific guidance toward goals that were based on the Common Core, College Board Advanced Placement or ISTE standards and that were aligned with the learning in each class.

By mid-year, students could articulate their growth and challenges in ways I had never experienced in my 13 years as an English teacher, and it wasn't only my most articulate students, it was all of them. Throwing out grades, regardless of the fact that I was functioning in a system that rejected the idea, was the best pedagogical decision I had made in a long time. There were many challenges and my execution wasn't perfect, but I did it, and one thing's for sure: I'll do it better every year moving forward.

Many people who participated in the process that year wanted me to write a book that answered all of their questions about getting rid of grades. That's what this is: a guide to help you create your own no-grades classroom. The book follows the *Hack Learning* format, so it will introduce problems we face with assessment, creative hacks, steps for immediate implementation, and a blueprint for building capacity. There will be some pointed commentary—some strong language. My attitude about grading may sound negative because, in my opinion, grading is negative. You'll read that "grades lie" because grades force students into categories that are imprecise and don't offer help for improvement.

I'll also address possible pushback. What will people say if they don't agree with the hack? First we'll explore the challenges and then I'll offer some responses to resolve the disagreement. Even with reasons and explanations, not everyone will get it, and that's okay. The most important thing to remember is that this is an ongoing process that will require some back and forth. Expect it.

Last, you'll see the hack in action. This section will provide anecdotes showing how the hack has worked in my setting as well as in other classrooms. These stories seek to show what a real no-grades classroom looks like, and here you'll find evidence to share with those who are more reluctant to embrace the idea of giving up grades.

Admittedly, making this change is not easy. You'll have challenges. You'll make mistakes. But communicating learning will become a conversation instead of a monologue: By giving narrative feedback and soliciting student input, we will make a significant impact on student learning.

HACK 1

SHIFT THE GRADES MINDSET

Start a no-grades classroom

The more we want our children to be (1) lifelong learners,
genuinely excited about words and numbers and ideas,
(2) avoid sticking with what's easy and safe, and (3)
become sophisticated thinkers, the more we should do
everything possible to help them forget about grades.
— ALFIE KOHN, AMERICAN AUTHOR/LECTURER

THE PROBLEM: THE TRADITIONAL GRADING SYSTEM

TRADITIONAL GRADING HAS been ingrained in American educational culture for more than a century. Because of the culture of grades that has emerged, we have lost sight of what is important in school: the learning. Too many students, parents, and educators focus excessively on labeling learning with numbers; they are willing to let that number or letter represent almost anything that can happen. Here are a few issues with traditional grading that must be hacked:

- Grades misrepresent what students know and can do because they oversimplify student achievement and categorize children into narrow boxes that stifle growth.

- Grades generate a competitive learning culture that de-emphasizes progress and pits students against each other. Since grades are often inflated with non-learning elements, they rarely demonstrate authentic or meaningful progress. Students then use the score they got on a test or a report card as an opportunity to claim they did better or know more than others, unaware that it is not an accurate representation of their ability. This is not an atmosphere that fosters risk taking.

- The language associated with grading often has a negative connotation that shuts the learning process down. Consider how it feels when a teacher tells a student he or she is wrong and draws a big "X" next to a child's work—that doesn't stimulate learning. Later in this chapter we will explore other language that can be adjusted to communicate effectively and positively.

THE HACK: SHIFT THE MINDSET AND THROW OUT GRADES

It's time to change the way we communicate about learning, and the most important step is to make sure all stakeholders understand why the shift is necessary. We need to help everyone involved, particularly students, understand that grades don't represent the depth of their understanding, that in fact grades are a short-sighted way to explore or to communicate about learning. Introducing a growth mindset, as Carol Dweck discusses in her book *Mindset*, is essential so students can evolve into successful learners—learners who are not quick

> Students must understand the various methods of feedback that their teacher and peers will provide and how to parlay that feedback into future growth.

to define themselves by letters or symbols that inadequately represent their learning.

Mindsets determine how we perceive the learning process. We must inspire students to focus on a growth mindset that allows for change and movement, rather than a fixed mindset that has the potential to stifle growth. When students earn C grades, they have a tendency to define themselves as "C students," often becoming stuck with this label. If we remove the label, we encourage students to see themselves simply as learners.

The shift to a growth mindset demands a corresponding shift in language to discuss the learning and assessing processes. Teachers must emphasize that there are multiple paths to learning and no one way is better than another. When students ask about grades, challenge them to think about learning. When we give students feedback, we aren't judging them; we are encouraging them to improve. This shift is an active one and will require vigilance on the part of the teacher and the learner.

WHAT YOU CAN DO TOMORROW

Transitioning away from traditional grades is a serious challenge, but there are several ways to ease the tension. Consider the following next steps:

- **Talk about going gradeless.** This discussion is essential: How you present it to students is going to determine how well they respond to the idea of eliminating grades. Begin by asking students what they think learning looks like. If they answer, "Doing all our work and getting A's," push back by asking more questions: "What do you get from doing all the work?" "What does it mean to get an A?"

  Although a strong work ethic is a valuable attribute that we want to instill in students, it doesn't define learning. You may ask them, "How many of you are afraid to fail?" If any raise their hands, ask, "What does failure mean?" It is essential that we develop a learning space where failure is positive, as it is a catalyst for growth and change. Students need to recognize that taking a risk and not succeeding does not mean they are failing: It means they need to try another way.

After posing the initial questions, break the class up into smaller groups to discuss the ideas that arose. See where the separate conversations take them and then bring them back to the whole class. Let students ask the questions. After all voices have been heard, end class with the opportunity to write about what they learned. What fears do they have about the upcoming year? How best can you help them transcend those fears? This will be their first reflection. While they write, so should you to show the value of the act and to model what will become a common practice.

If time permits, ask volunteers to read their reflections. Then share yours. Make a space in the classroom to post reflections as a reminder throughout the year. Let this be the beginning of a very important discussion that will not end in one day, but will continue all year long.

Talk about mastery learning. Initially, students may be able to wrap their brains around the idea, but how this new process actually looks will feel like a mystery. Dispel the uncertainty by providing concrete examples of mastery learning. Discuss what it was like when they learned to ride a bike. The first time they tried, they may have failed; they may have fallen off the bike many times, but they kept getting up and trying again. Some may have started with training wheels, which is comparable to approaching proficiency; they could do it with help. Once they could ride without training wheels or help, they had reached proficiency. After they had been riding awhile and could go on rides for long distances or could ride different bikes, they had achieved mastery. You can then take this pattern and apply it to something students are learning.

A BLUEPRINT FOR FULL IMPLEMENTATION

Step 1: Continue the dialogue throughout the year.

Just because you had the conversation once doesn't mean it's over. Expect to have ongoing discussions about this concept all year long. Try not to get frustrated or exasperated when students need more time to take it in. They will continue to ask what they "got" on something and it will be your job to redirect the conversation—take the opportunity to remind them that learning has no grades. Instead ask them, "What did you learn from that assignment? What could you do now that you couldn't do before? How do you know?" Students will come to expect the redirection until they have internalized the shift.

Step 2: Routinely review and clarify the standards of learning.

Make sure students understand class learning expectations (not rules) and standards. Have students translate expectations and standards into student-friendly language and internalize them; then, ask each student to determine his or her level of proficiency based on mastery of the standards. Since standards are often written in a language students don't readily understand, it will take time to build a vocabulary and understanding of learning and each subject will require a specific jargon.

One way to help students know what they don't know is by asking them to apply skills and knowledge to new situations without help. When they have reached mastery level, they can take what they know from one place and apply it appropriately to another without prompting, creating and synthesizing new ideas. Encourage students to generate and track short-term and long-term goals. Remind them that they are in control of their learning. In the spirit of effective differentiation, each child may be working on different outcomes within a unit at different times. Allowing them to determine their pace and skill will support future buy-in.

Step 3: Create and share feedback models regularly.

Exemplars will be your friend throughout the year, but even the best samples of last year's work will need to be updated. (See the example at the end of this hack.) Students must understand the various methods of feedback that their teacher and peers will provide and how to parlay that feedback into future growth. For example, they will have opportunities to receive written feedback on work, to engage in short conversations during group projects, or to have one-on-one discussions that include specific strategies about different aspects of their learning. They will also be providing feedback to you about what works best for them.

Step 4: Change the vocabulary associated with learning.

Traditional grading language is passive and is often negative, so we can shift the way we talk about assessment. Instead of using the words "grade" or "grading," use "assessment" or "assessing." We must be conscious of our diction, as our words characterize our thinking and communicate attitude: One simple word change can affect the connotation drastically.

Grades vocabulary	No-grades vocabulary
grading	assessing
score	assess
"What grade did I get?"	"What did I learn?"
"This is wrong."	"Try another way."
problem	challenge, opportunity
judgment or criticism	feedback
get good grades	achieve proficiency or mastery

OVERCOMING PUSHBACK

Some students may not like giving up grades because they have defined themselves in reference to these numbers and letters their whole lives. The more academically inclined the student is, the more reluctant he or she may be to relinquish the numbers and letters that make him or her feel smart. The parents of such a student will also likely make the shift more challenging (we'll get to this in Hack 2).

Students and parents won't understand this shift; they are used to grades. Let's face it, this system is the only one they know and it's validated by the fact that parents understand it and have instilled in their children that getting good grades is equal to success. Of course they do really want their kids to learn and generally will agree that learning is more important than the grade, so you will need to be patient. The best way to overcome this fixed mindset is to continue to have conversations and share the reasons you've eliminated grades and the value of assessment based on narrative feedback and self-evaluation.

Be strong. The system won't change overnight; it will take time and many people making the conscious shift together. If you can get the whole school on board, that will greatly increase the likelihood of success with parents and students.

The unknown is very scary and therefore it won't work. Many people will say that they don't understand and are uncomfortable with the idea of doing something unknown, particularly if you are switching the system students are using toward the end of their secondary experience. They will worry about transcripts and report cards and college applications. You must reiterate that ultimately they will have all of those things—it's just that their evaluation will involve a new process that encourages their involvement and requires them to take charge of their own learning. Remind them, console them, and help them understand that change is challenging, but that doesn't mean it isn't worthwhile. Don't be afraid to hold their hands until you gain their trust. There will be times when the need for a whole class discussion will take priority over scheduled plans or when students need a one-on-one chat, so be flexible and patient.

Why change a system that isn't broken? Some folks won't like this idea, simply because they adhere to the *status quo*: "This is the way we've always done it and it isn't broken!" Counter this argument with history: In the industrial era, schools were intended to train good workers, so students went to schools that prepared them to enter the work force. This model of education valued obedience, conformity, and rote learning. From there you can discuss how much the world has changed in the last hundred years and generate a list of ways that a 19th-century system doesn't prepare kids for the creativity and critical thinking required of the 21st century.

THE HACK IN ACTION

At the beginning of my AP Literature and Composition class, I sent a letter home to parents explaining this essential shift in philosophy and practice about communicating learning. It didn't seem like many of them read it, as no one sent me any confirmation. Most likely, parents cast it off with the other "unimportant" notices that go home senior year, but I wasn't discouraged: My mind was made up.

"How am I going to know that I'm doing well if you don't give us grades?" This question was on repeat for quite some time, but I assured students that we would be working on that together, first by making sure that the standards and expectations were clear, then by examining examples of mastery work and using frequent feedback.

For example, the first unit of the year was an exploration of poetry that focused on getting students to consider how a poem functions rather than what it means. Students were tasked with creating a tutorial about a particular poetic device or structure to be shared with their classmates. The assignment required students to research a poetic device, find examples of the device in poems, and then determine the best way to teach the material so their audience would learn it. They had two weeks in class to research and produce the tutorial; at the same time, we were doing whole class mini-lessons on the best way to accomplish these tasks.

Once students selected their groups, I met with each group to hear their ideas. I helped them to ensure that they stayed on target and presented accurate information. This feedback was intended to troubleshoot with them, not to provide answers, so I bounced questions and ideas off them, pointing them in the right direction. Part of the project's purpose was for students to discover knowledge on their own.

While they worked, I was not only discussing progress, but was also observing group dynamics to see that all students were contributing. It's important that each student receives individual feedback—the days of providing one group grade are over. I used to do it, but have changed my practice since reading Susan M. Brookhart's book *Grading and Group Work,* which convinced me to assess students' work individually.

Once students completed the project, we did a gallery walk: All of the projects were set up around the room on computers, and small groups moved around the room viewing the projects, taking notes, and tweeting questions and comments. They reviewed each group's tutorial and provided feedback based on the standards using a Google form. Every student was required to submit a reflection and self-evaluation about what he or she learned as compared against the standards so that we could discuss growth. Students reflected on what they had hoped to get out of the assignment and then shared what they had learned.

After this process, some students continued to ask what they "got" or what I thought of their assignments, but I steadfastly replied, "It doesn't really matter what I thought, so much as it matters what you learned. What did you learn from this learning experience?" At the beginning of the year, I frequently had to redirect students in this way. The true test of the system's efficacy, however, was when it came time for them to write their first poetry analysis paper, a two- to three-page unresearched paper that asked them to apply the skills they had learned from the tutorials.

It wasn't until after they wrote the paper that they began to recognize how much they had learned. In their reflections, I saw responses like, "I was able to use what we did in our group tutorial to help make sense of my poem, and that met this standard." When students discussed their learning in an articulate and meaningful way, I knew they were starting to understand the value of the procedures we were using.

Eventually students told me that not worrying about grades made them more excited and eager to try things. Although they didn't realize it yet, they had been like this when they were younger, before they were afraid of being wrong. By the end of the year, they saw the connection and recognized that the shift away from grades was worth the time and effort.

The success of the shift away from grades will come only from a full commitment to helping each child learn without labels. Although challenges will present themselves, both internally and externally, we must embrace the fact that growth is possible in everyone and it shouldn't be tracked with scores: Those numbers and letters impede progress and stifle potential. Consider your own impact in the classroom. What do you do to model this mindset and what can you change personally to generate a more inclusive community in your space?

HACK 2

PROMOTE BUY-IN

Open lines of communication with stakeholders

The question, then, is not about changing people; it's about reaching people. I'm not speaking simply of better information, a sharper and clearer factual presentation to disperse the thick fogs generated by today's spin machines.
— BILL MOYERS, AMERICAN JOURNALIST AND POLITICAL COMMENTATOR

THE PROBLEM: STAKEHOLDERS ARE RELUCTANT TO CHANGE

WHEN MAKING A big change like throwing out grades, many people will not "get it" and may push back in ways that impede the progress of students. Schools and colleges have supported the traditional grading system for far too long, making it challenging to suggest this seemingly radical, but important, reform.

THE HACK: PROMOTE BUY-IN FOR THROWING OUT TRADITIONAL GRADES

To ensure optimal impact on student learning, every stakeholder needs to be involved and must support the cause. Students need to hear the same message from all of their teachers—a message that is supported by administration and further supported by their greatest advocates, their parents. Shifting students' mindsets is challenging; getting adults to reconsider theirs is much more challenging but not impossible.

To align the school message, several things will need to happen. One is peer-to-peer conversations with colleagues who are receptive to new ideas. Staff learning opportunities will ensure that practice is well informed and consistent. Teachers will need support from administrators, who will also need resources to properly implement such a big change in communication.

Be specific when discussing why this change must happen with the adults involved. Once the "why" is evident, you can work on a plan for the "how" that best suits your individual school community. It's important to consider the size of the school and age level of the learners as you begin to make these decisions.

WHAT YOU CAN DO TOMORROW

Adults can be closed-minded when they are comfortable with the *status quo*, so you'll have to give them evidence that this new way is better. Assuming you are at the beginning of the process, consider the following:

- **Suggest resources that promote change.** Share a few resources about shifting away from grades that will resonate with colleagues and administrators. These can be books, blog posts, podcasts, Twitter streams, or Facebook groups, like #TTOG and Teachers Throwing Out Grades, respectively. Refer to the Resources page at the end of this book for a list of recommendations.

- **Provide examples.** Illustrate how student learning has improved with this new method. If you have students who can talk about it, even better. Bring students with you when you have an

informal peer conversation or a more formal faculty meeting.
Encourage them to explain how shifting away from grades
helps them become self-evaluative, independent learners.

Present classroom action research findings. Prove to colleagues and administrators that the system works, then ask about
starting a committee for optimal implementation. For now, just
drop in for an informal conversation to get the temperature of the
situation at your school. If you can gather a few "beta" testers with
you, they will strengthen your case.

Write a letter to parents. Explain the shift in methodology
and encourage parents to provide feedback and inquiry as an
ongoing practice.

Set up a class Twitter hashtag. A unique hashtag creates a
virtual space that aggregates any tweet about your class or assessment system. This can be an easy way to collect questions, concerns, and comments in one location to develop a dialogue with
parents and community stakeholders.

Sign up for a YouTube account. Once you set up a YouTube
channel, begin planning videos that will keep parents informed.

A BLUEPRINT FOR FULL IMPLEMENTATION

Step 1: Meet with administrators to discuss the shift.

This kind of change will require the support of administration, so
list the many benefits of making the change and be prepared with
talking points when you go in. Administrators don't have the time to
do the research—make sure you provide it for them.

Explain the benefits for students and how throwing out grades
will enhance the learning experience. The more detailed your talking
points, the more likely you are to garner support. Use the different

hacks in this book as talking points to help administration under-stand how necessary these changes are.

Step 2: Conduct a professional learning session.

Gather staff members and communicate the philosophy the same way you did with students. Make sure to have research and student outcomes ready to share. Invite questions, and if you can't answer them imme-diately, provide an answer within 24 hours. Create a multimedia pre-sentation with student messages and/or video that demonstrates what feedback in your classroom looks like.

Step 3: Invite parents in to discuss the change.

Help parents envision how using feedback instead of grades will make communication about learning better. If you're using an online grading system, make sure they know and understand the symbols you are using. Honor the questions they have about the change and be patient. In your information letter, invite them to follow class progress on Twitter using the class hashtag and on YouTube by watching your videos. Continue to engage in conversations via email, phone calls, and social media until all par-ents are comfortable with the shift.

> It isn't the grade but the conversation that communicates the learning.

Step 4: Involve the parent coordinator in the process.

If you're fortunate enough to have a parent coordinator or a PTA pres-ident at your school, enlist the help of that person. Spend time helping him or her understand the shift so you will have a liaison to support your cause when you aren't there to discuss the change with parents. This person can be a strong ally, someone you'll want on your side.

Step 5: Support the staff.

One learning session isn't going to be enough to roll out this change successfully. You'll need ongoing support. Make sure you cover topics like using no-grading vocabulary, providing meaningful feedback, offering opportunities to revise and redo, understanding mastery learning, valuing engagement over compliance, and other issues that often get mixed up while assessing student achievement.

Step 6: Establish a school-wide initiative.

Once early adopters are on board, you'll need a strategy that implements the changes in a relatively systematic and consistent way. The school staff should determine policies together to ensure minimal confusion during the transition.

Step 7: Create a beta team to try it out first.

The whole school may not be ready right away. Instead of jumping in without seeing how the system will work, consider having a small group do it first. Perhaps approach a grade level team or a department; preferably it should be a group of teachers who share the same students. This way the students have a consistent experience and the teachers can solve problems together.

Step 8: Full school implementation.

Once the beta testing and research are done and the staff and community have been informed appropriately, it's time for a school-wide shift. It will be easier to implement the changes when everyone has been briefed and prepared and each voice and concern has been heard. Put a committee in place with the original beta team and some other teachers, administrators, and parents who want to help ensure progress. Keep it positive and keep moving forward.

Step 9: Check in with the stakeholders.

Periodically check the climate. How are people feeling about the shift? What can you do to support them better? You may want to create a quick Google form to make sure that you're meeting everyone's needs (see Figure 2.1).

Figure 2.1

OVERCOMING PUSHBACK

Change is hard and the people we work most closely with can be our greatest challenges, so you'll need to be prepared for some resistance.

Tracking progress for all my students will be overwhelming. No one will argue that tracking progress is not time consuming, but the amount and quality of tracking can markedly increase the amount and quality of student learning. Throughout this book, you will find useful strategies for reducing the constraints on a teacher's time. Remember, providing narrative feedback about learning and encouraging self-evaluation are the most important parts of a no-grades classroom, so the time you invest will pay huge dividends throughout the year.

Kids aren't motivated to work without grades. Believe it or not, kids are only motivated by grades because grades are the only carrot students know. If we can help students become intrinsically motivated, then the grade at the end is not significant. Attention gets focused on the learning, not on how we communicate the learning. Using grades as a motivator doesn't encourage learning on a larger scale; it merely motivates in the short term. Grades ultimately end up being a power tool that serves the teacher but not the student. It's important to explain this to students and repeat the lesson throughout the year. Remind students that they are not letters or numbers. They are lifelong learners.

Students can't get into college without grades. Many home-schooled students get into college without grades, so there are schools that accept portfolios over transcripts. Many university and community colleges also accept students from other countries that use variations on letter or number grades or GPAs. However, for schools that require transcripts and grades, students will be taught to self-grade and that final term grade will appear on a transcript. In fact, last year all of my students who applied got into college. I just received a thank you email from a recently graduated senior who started college over the summer. She shared that the reflective practices she learned helped her be better prepared for her college classes.

How will I know how my child is doing? Students will have greater ability to articulate what they know and can do in the no-grades class-room. When they discuss their learning, they will be able to point to the level of mastery in the work, which is a better indication of what they have learned than a grade. It isn't the *grade* but the *conversation* that communicates the learning. Parents will still be able to talk to teachers about specific areas of strength and challenges and how they can be involved in helping their child improve. Parents will now have descriptive feedback and volumes of work samples that will surely be more accurate and informative than a single letter or number.

THE HACK IN ACTION

Sarah Donovan is a teacher who is in the process of transitioning to a no-grades classroom. Here, she provides an excellent example of how to approach a principal when you are ready to begin the process.

> In 2013 our junior high school unblocked English Language Arts (ELA). Separating reading and writing allowed for greater flexibility in scheduling, but it also made writing an inclusive class. Typically, students with low test scores would be put into a reading intervention class, which did not focus on writing skills. In decoupling these literacy strands, teachers learned how to facilitate writing workshop, a method emphasizing process over product.
>
> Naturally, there was less grading and more feedback in these writing classes. And naturally, this led our department to notice how while we were talking less about grades, the grades actually went up. In other words, by not focusing on grades, there was more learning and achievement. Of course, we still gave grades, but the irony of putting a letter or point value on the process was not lost on us.
>
> When our administrators looked at GPAs, they also noticed that writing grades were typically higher than reading grades. Literacy skills aside for the moment, our conversations pointed to the key differences as practice and

assessment. In the writing classes, the practice was happening mostly in class, and the assessment was formative, encouraging students to revise and resubmit. Learning was more conversational. Yes, in reading class, we discussed literature, but much of the reading was happening outside of class (as homework), and the assessments were typically graded. The grade ended the conversation.

The GPA conversation prompted the (then) principal to start a committee on school grading practices. This didn't really take off. Grades are a tradition in schools. The "A" and a high GPA have been at the heart of many motivational speeches in our classrooms and assemblies (along with "do your homework" and "no excuses"). However, just inviting teachers to rethink grading prompted some people to ask for resources and reflect on their practices. I started doing some research.

This year, while supervising eighth-grade graduation practice, I walked around with Mark Barnes's book *Assessment 3.0*, which advocates a no-grades classroom. Teachers were stopping me to ask about it, so I told them I'd pass along what I learned. I had always used narrative feedback and portfolios, but I had not considered even asking if I could do away with grades. *Assessment 3.0* helped me to imagine "what if," so I decided to put together a proposal for a no-grades classroom.

A couple of weeks into summer school, I had a sample letter to parents with a rationale for a feedback approach to assessment, a plan for documenting written and verbal feedback (blogs, notebooks, charts), and an outline of how end-of-quarter conferences might look (portfolio, standards, reflection). Then, I made an appointment with our new principal.

We met one afternoon after summer school. I started by reflecting on our discussions related to GPA and how our conversations with students and teachers focused on getting grades up rather than learning. We targeted students based on their low GPAs and then pulled them out of lunch or class to talk to them about getting grades up, doing assignments, filling in those zeros. Essentially, we were talking to students about a system that they had no control over, a system that was rather arbitrary. This teacher allowed late work, this teacher didn't; this teacher used zeros, this teacher didn't. If we didn't have grades, what would those conversations have looked like?

He listened carefully. We had recently purchased a computer program that would take us in the direction of standards-based grading, so he wanted to know how a no-grades classroom might work with that program and how it would fit with standards-based teaching practices. I didn't have the answers, but I knew I would use the standards as a way of setting up activities and guiding feedback. I knew I would want students to look at the standards at the end of the quarter and say, "Look at this blog post comparing *A Book Thief* and *Night*. I compare a fictional and historical account of the holocaust for how they account for their place in the 1940s. I even use proper MLA citation. Look."

This all seemed reasonable to him. He is a reasonable guy but had three key concerns:

- **Final grades:** We talked about how we could probably get away without midterm grades, but the district required quarterly grades. He wanted to know how we would decide on a final, quarter grade. I talked to him about Barnes's final grade conference and how the grade would emerge from a grade conference.

- **Parents:** He wanted to know how I would communicate progress to parents. I thought about this, and I knew the class blog would be a record of my feedback and the student responding to the feedback. Parents could see this any time. Still, how would I indicate where students were in the assessment process if students were in the process of resubmitting something or if they hadn't done it in the first place? I thought I'd have to make use of the school-wide grading program somehow. So we talked about developing a code to communicate with students and parents to make the process transparent.

- **Colleagues:** What would they think of this? How would my no-grades classroom work alongside a classroom with a more traditional approach? I had not really thought of that. I knew there were a few teachers eager to do more feedback, to rethink zeros and late work, but was he saying that this change might cause animosity or divisions among the faculty? My response was simply that I'd try to make the process transparent and talk about it as one way of rethinking grading.

Changing a system like grades is not something that can be done with a few weeks of research. Grades are part of the institution of school, and our beliefs about learning and achievement are bound up in those letters. What I am doing, and some of my colleagues are joining me, is rethinking a system that has alienated a lot of students in our Title I school. As an ELA teacher, I do think that words are powerful, so I am starting by changing the language we use to talk about learning.

Although full buy-in from all stakeholders is ideal, it is unlikely. There will always be someone who is unsatisfied or doesn't agree, but try not to worry about that person too much. Engage in a dialogue that focuses on facts and spend your energy where it counts, on the folks who do get it and want to support teachers and students. Consider your school community. Who will be your early adopters? How can you use their support to engage the larger community? Who will give the biggest pushback? In what ways can you turn those negatives into positives?

HACK 3

REBRAND ASSIGNMENTS AS LEARNING EXPERIENCES

Design comprehensive projects for optimal growth

Teaching is no longer about relaying the content
standard... it's about transforming lives.

— DAVE BURGESS, AUTHOR/EDUCATOR

THE PROBLEM: ASSIGNMENTS DON'T PROVIDE AMPLE OPPORTUNITY TO SHOW LEARNING

TOO MANY TESTS and assignments offer little in the way of creativity and student growth. Some teachers use the same activities from year to year to make grading easier. It's an unfortunate reality that projects or tests seldom get revised to really develop students as learners. Instead, they offer ample opportunity to be right or wrong, which can dampen a love of learning. There are several problems with these assignments and assessments:

- Many tests and projects don't allow for students to show depth of learning.

- When teachers don't allow iteration, this stunts student growth.

- Most assignments provide a single path to learning, taking away student autonomy.

THE HACK: MAKE INSTRUCTION A FORMATIVE EXPERIENCE

Every assignment, project, or classroom experience must support a progressive movement in every child's learning. The teacher should consider deliberate ways to make all learning substantial and to connect content and skill to what is relevant in students' lives.

Teachers need to involve students in choices and provide opportunities for them to modify a teacher's assignments or to create their own. When we say "Yes" to student ideas, we encourage autonomy and empower them. Giving our students a voice in instruction and assessment develops a collaborative relationship that ultimately enhances achievement.

In addition to collaborating with students and giving them a voice, teachers need to consider multimodal opportunities that extend learning and differentiate for every child. With ample time and feedback, students can revise original work, practicing essential skills that will propel them to mastery.

WHAT YOU CAN DO TOMORROW

It's time we start asking kids about their learning preferences. The more we include students in the process of creating learning experiences, the better the outcomes will be. Here are some easy ways to rebrand assignments as ongoing learning experiences.

Poll your students. It's important that teachers understand what students like about learning. This can be as simple as asking kids to raise their hands after a series of questions and recording their answers or collecting a piece of paper with their ideas; or it can be as high-tech as creating a simple survey online. A few easy-to-use apps or websites are Poll Everywhere, Plicker, SurveyMonkey, and Socrative. Ask a few simple questions including, "How do you like to learn?" The goal is to find out how each student's voice will contribute to the feedback loop, when activities are created later.

Practice revising part of a project or a piece of writing. Take what you're currently working on, provide peer or teacher feedback, and allow the student to continue working on the assignment to improve it. Explain how this facilitates ongoing learning. Invite students to consider what they're doing and how they might proceed. Remind students that their decisions help drive their learning.

Adjust assignments for particular student needs. In an existing assignment, work with students to adjust expectations to ensure that all children can be successful. This is a good place to honor student input. This can be done in a variety of ways that do not consume too much time. For example, you might share a list of guidelines and invite students to identify parts they don't understand and to explain how they might approach particular directions. They can respond in a notebook or on a blog or other web-based tool. This activity amplifies student voice and encourages self-evaluation.

Say Yes to a student-generated idea. If a student asks you to do something in place of an existing assignment, before you say no, ask to hear the idea and help to adjust it so that it meets the same criteria as the original assignment. Optionally, this can be a class assignment. Explain a learning outcome and invite students to brainstorm ways they can demonstrate mastery.

A BLUEPRINT FOR FULL IMPLEMENTATION

Step 1: Revise your curriculum with the help of students.

Examine the curriculum with your students, bearing in mind what must be covered. Take an inventory of the current curriculum and explore what can be changed, adjusted, left out, or put in; rebuild it for maximum student engagement. Remind them that assignments are being rebranded as learning experiences that include student voice.

Step 2: Align projects with specific skills or standards.

Knowing your end point is essential before you begin, so make sure that all assignments are purposeful and aligned to a standard. Review what must be accomplished by the end of the year, create the assessments, and then plan backwards to the beginning of the course. It may help to start with a skeleton of the whole thing and fill in the details topic by topic. Ask yourself if your project is truly a learning experience that involves student autonomy, facilitates a feedback loop, and will be enjoyable.

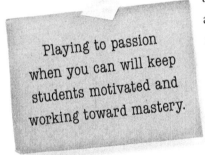

Playing to passion when you can will keep students motivated and working toward mastery.

Step 3: Teach students to understand the standards.

It's not enough just to tell students the standard or place it on an assignment sheet. Students must be able to internalize it. Consider using an activity that asks students to reconstruct or rewrite the standards for each unit. Taking time to complete this activity prior to a unit or major project helps students envision the depth and breadth of the work, while considering what they need to accomplish. Here are a few tips for this important activity:

1. Explain what the standards are and what role they will play in the learning experience.

2. Inform students that they will be rewriting the standards in a language they understand. Instruct them to translate the standards into student-friendly language on sentence strips or chart paper.

3. Model the process with the first standard or learning outcome. Read it aloud, and then break it apart phrase-by-phrase or word-by-word. Rewrite it in simple language. Think aloud while you rewrite the standard.

4. Instruct students to repeat the process with a different standard. Leave the model and samples on the board or chart paper for the class to see while they work in groups.

5. Divide students into groups of two to three and assign them three to five standards per group.

6. Have students present the new standards in their own words in a way that works for them.

7. Create an evolving bulletin board with the rewritten standards so students can refer to them throughout the year.

8. Ask students to decide which standards they are meeting while they are working and during reflection time.

As we continue to teach kids to reflect, we must remind them to reference the standards and to explain how they are addressing them in their work. This will help shift the conversation away from grades and keep it where it needs to be: on learning.

Step 4: Build choice into learning experience.

Many sources indicate that allowing for student choice increases student engagement (see the Resources section at the end of this book). Wherever reasonable and possible, allow choice for students. Give them options or allow them to generate new possibilities of their own. Throughout the year, when introducing new content, always ask, "How can you demonstrate mastery of this concept or skill?" Don't let students shrug this off; remind them that you've rebranded assignments to learning experiences that always give students a voice.

Step 5: Tap into student passions.

Know your students well so you can appeal to their interests. One year, a group of students loved to perform and create skits. My previous year's students didn't enjoy these kinds of activities; they wanted more technology. Of course, you will need to balance everything out, but playing to passion when you can will keep students motivated and working toward mastery. Remember, you can't rebrand assignments and ignore what students enjoy.

Step 6: Connect content and skills throughout the year.

As students are learning new material, it is essential that new work encourages them to recall and apply the skills and content they learned earlier in the year. Continued practice and application in new situations will deepen understanding and help students progress toward mastery. Always ask students how something they learned earlier is helping them learn something new. Reminding students of the value of prior learning will help facilitate ongoing feedback and self-assessment. Figure 3.1 provides one example of how teachers can help students connect skills and reflect on their own learning.

Mixed Media - Final Project - Choose your own adventure

This year you will be selecting and creating your own final assessment. You will create your assignment, the format in which you want to present it and the content you want to work with related to journalism.

Phase 1 - Selecting a topic and/or mode to do the project in. **Due 4/24**

Column A - Topics	Column B - Mode
journalism ethics photojournalism coverage of any major event journalism history technology	investigative feature photo essay series of short form pieces podcast video scrapbook/yearbook style

Phase 2 - Writing an assignment sheet - You will submit a formal assignment sheet for me to understand what your project is. You will have time in class to complete this. Your final draft will be due via google docs on **due 5/2**
- all assignments MUST have multiple elements
- all assignments MUST include at least 2 interviews to gather information
- all assignments MUST include secondary research of some kind
- all assignments MUST have a written AND visual element

Phase 3 - a Formal mode of assessment (rubric, checklist with standards, scale, etc) **due on 5/9**
- all assessments MUST be based on the common core standards: http://www.corestandards.org/
- all assignments must explicitly tell what success indicators are

Phase 4 - Work on your project in class - students must schedule conference time along the way - **due 5/31**
- You will create a timeline appropriate for your work schedule in class and share it with me (actually written down)
- create benchmarks to help manage your time

Phase 5 - Reflection - standards based reflection on your learning experience - beginning to end due **6/3**
- Reference learning to standards
- be in essay form - single spaced
- grade yourself and justify it

Phase 6 - Presentation - you will be presenting about your experience. due **June 3rd - Monday - More on this to follow as it gets closer**

Phase 7 - Eportfolio uploading due **June 3rd**

Figure 3.1

Step 7: Always provide options for students to create their own path to learning.

Once students are used to being a part of the creation process, you should consider opening all projects and assignments up to a student design option. They will learn right away that this is not easier, but in fact more challenging, because they will need to consider what they must accomplish before they start. Being a teacher/creator is at the highest level of Bloom's Taxonomy and will allow students to demonstrate mastery.

OVERCOMING PUSHBACK

Traditionally, school has been full of worksheets and teacher-driven tests and assignments. Although we know these practices are misguided, some teachers still use them. Here are some of the things you may hear from colleagues, students, or parents about rebranding assignments:

49

These kinds of assignments are too subjective. Creative assignments allow students rather than teachers to make the rules and to determine what is quality work, and this makes some people very uncomfortable. However, there is seldom only one right way to do anything. We need to provide opportunities for creativity while students synthesize learning, encouraging them to do things in a way that is intuitive. All learning is subjective, and when we only offer one chance or route for learning, we greatly limit the possibility that every student will achieve mastery.

There isn't enough time to allow students to work in class. Time is always going to be a challenge, but many skills can be taught through the process of working on longer, more complicated assignments, rather than shorter "one and done" assignments. If we adjust the way we spend our class time, then it is entirely possible to allow students to do the work in front of us rather than at home. Teachers will no longer spend full periods lecturing: This is not an efficient use of class time if students are to master content effectively. Employing effective collaboration and technology integration will alleviate time constraints, allowing the teacher to become more of a coach and a facilitator.

There is too much content to cover in my class to teach this way. As with the challenge above, we must put depth of understanding before breadth of coverage. If students don't understand content that we "gloss over," then we do them no service by mentioning all of the topics they need for an exam. Consider the order in which concepts are presented and overlap and incorporate as much as is reasonable in each assignment. Allowing students to practice skills and develop competencies is a more effective use of time than presenting PowerPoints crammed with content.

Projects don't prepare students for tests. Any good test will not ask for rote memorization. Life isn't a test with predetermined questions and answers; we need to teach kids to attack and solve problems using their knowledge and skills. Projects most definitely prepare our students because projects help students learn how to apply knowledge and use skills in different settings. If students are prepared for life by having mastered educational standards in a variety of settings and challenges, they should excel at any valid test.

THE HACK IN ACTION

Synthesis projects present students with a problem and require them to collaborate to develop a solution, all the while developing skills and learning new concepts. One example of a synthesis project assignment sheet can be seen in Figure 3.2.

Sackstein's Satirical Expectations
a re-interpretation of the classics

Directions: in small groups, you will highlight elements from any or all of the literature read so far this year. You will make a short movie (no more than 10 minutes) satirizing these key moments you select making sure to draw on the challenges of reading these novels in today's society. Using humor and irony and sense of your group's understanding of the novel, create this movie with specific references to the text. (You may update the language as needed).

Steps to completion and further expectations
- select which element you want to focus on: character development, plot structure or setting
- select which key elements from each text
- develop an angle to tell your new story based on these elements from the modern perspective
- write a script (you will need to produce this to turn in with the movie) with all direction on it
- film the movie
- upload to youtube or vimeo and share the link with me
- each member of the group should write a reflection that addresses the process, learning, team dynamics and standards addressed... successes and challenges and what you might do differently next time
- upload all work onto e-portfolio
- on due date DECEMBER 18th - all elements should be emailed before class... your video should also be on a jump drive so we can view them in class.
  - (you will be submitting:
    - 1 script for the group.
    - 1 movie for the group.
    - 4 reflections (1 from each member of the group).
    - All should be uploaded onto e-portfolio

Figure 3.2

Students consistently use these project experiences to grow as learners. Of course, other ways of learning, such as writing essays, are necessary in high school; however, they don't have to be completed, isolated activities that lack process.

Here's how Aric Foster, a high school English teacher and no-grades classroom advocate, rebrands assignments, making learning experiences out of essay writing for AP exams.

> "As soon as we put a number on student work, learning stops." After hearing this in the Twittersphere, I was inspired to make changes to my own grading practices. While I have been using standards-based learning for years, I felt like even the labels of 4.0-1.0 stagnated the feedback loop. It is every teacher's dream that learners receive feedback, internalize it into their souls, and then grow in proficiency from this feedback to never repeat the same miscue again. While this is rarely the case, amending how I cultivate the feedback loop has made noticeable strides in achieving this learning Utopia.
>
> The most prominent example for me came when I changed how I assess my AP Literature students when they wrote AP essays. I have used many different rubrics to assess this crucial task—all of which were blatantly tied to standards and clearly delineated levels of proficiency in those standards. In addition, learners logged the written feedback I gave them in an attempt to make it more meaningful. However, it wasn't until I moved from a numbered rubric to a "feedback only" form that I saw drastic improvement in student writing.
>
> Figure 3.3 was inspired by Mark Barnes's SE2R feedback model. Barnes suggests that feedback be given as follows: summarize, explain, redirect, resubmit. When a student submits an essay, I merely record what I see, how the work does or does not address standards, resources to pursue to amend areas of concern, and a new plan for resubmitting the work.

TTOG Feedback

Mr. Foster will fill this out as your "rubric" for tasks. When you complete the resubmission below, attach this sheet. Be sure to add amendments and/or disagreements to Mr. Foster's comments on this sheet when you resubmit.

Student:

Task:

Code	Feedback
Boxes around words	Strong or weak diction = **color** stylistic authorship
Squiggly line under words/phrases	Grammatical error = **black/white** mechanics
ATR/HOW/A?	Make the path (author's ideas → texts words/literary devices → effect on the reader) clear; explain HOW the author created meaning; answer the AP question using specific text evidence = **How/answer the question**

Foster saw:

Foster didn't see:

How this shows proficiency, or lack thereof, in learning target(s):

Extra practice to address areas of concern:

Resubmission:

Figure 3.3

My goals are to keep my comments as objective as possible, to notice and coach while not judging harshly or praising superfluously, to help learners see how their work adheres to an established norm of proficiency. I have found that this process not only builds a culture of learning but encourages learners to take risks and challenge themselves, as they know there will be no punitive words or numbers for their performance—only observations and suggestions for revision.

This process, this rebranding, fosters a paradigm shift, both for the learners and for me. No longer are learners trying to earn points or "get a 3.0." Instead, they are trying to *Answer the Question* and *Use Style* and *Cite Evidence to Support a Claim* and basically just write better. Evidence-based learning helped my learners shift the focus from "playing school" to "achieving a standard." However, when I threw out grades completely and purged classwork of numbers to achieve, my students started to learn for the sake of learning. They began to attempt class work with a new mindset—one of collegiality and growth, not compliance and immobility.

From my point of view as the teacher, this alteration revised how I think about work in class as well. Before this revolution, I was a teacher who was conducting a lesson and almost formulaically circling numbers on a rubric that matched what a learner produced. While that is not a harmful practice and does cultivate growth and does adhere to standards, it is still just teaching. Instead, now I consider myself a coach. A coach sees how his "athletes" performed, analyzes how that performance is what we are all looking for, and provides resources and encouragement and practice to perform even better. Rather than wearing the tie of a teacher, I now have a whistle, game film, and drills we can practice in order to do better in the next big game.

Also, by coaching and not just teaching, I can more easily see areas where my coaching is lacking. This year, after following this "feedback only" process, it was clearly evident that I was struggling to teach *Answering the Question* effectively. So what did I do? I did the same feedback process: I noticed my deficiency, sought resources to improve (Twitter, Voxer, professional development, etc.), and "resubmitted" my work by amending future lessons. This rebranding facilitates a culture of learning for my students, allows me to help individual students learn more meaningfully, and provides an avenue for me to do continuous professional growth.

I remember this was especially meaningful for "Clare" last year. Clare was pushing herself even by enrolling in the AP class and struggled repeatedly at the beginning of the year to produce up to the AP standard. For her first essay, the feedback I gave her followed the aforementioned feedback process:

<u>What I saw</u>: "I see that you have only one transition in the whole essay and that you cited only one example from the

text to prove your thesis. I also see that you effectively used three of our vocabulary words and did not have any grammatical errors that distracted from meaning."

Addressing standards: "Using mature and varied transitions to move from one idea to the next shows proficiency in our *Style* standard and explaining how multiple examples from the text prove a thesis shows proficiency in our *Answer the Question* standard."

Resources: "Please read three other student essays, highlight all of the transitions you see, and tell me what you found. Also, please review our AP notes about 'How to answer the question' and tell me which strategy you plan to use."

Resubmission: Revise your second paragraph to address these areas of concern. Highlight your *Style* amendments in green and *Answer the Question* amendments in pink."

Clare then sought multiple avenues to succeed: coursework, classmates' products, and coaching from me. Her resubmission is potent, clearly delineates the standards she addressed, and makes it easy for me to see if and how she addressed the areas of concern.

Yes, it might seem like this is "a lot of work" and impractical for the teacher to do for every assignment, every time. However, this is where the learning happens. This is why the learners and I are in the same room together.

"Pass back paper day" used to be a 10-minute lesson in my room where I mentioned a few common errors to the entire class. Now, this is an entire class period where students are working with each other to see examples of how they can amend their own work, consulting resources to improve their proficiency, and conferring with me to clarify how to develop their writing. I am not spending time putting numbers in a grade book or circling boxes on a rubric; I am using my time more effectively and potently to address student learning.

Oh, and Clare? She earned a 3 on the AP test.

To achieve optimal growth, students need to be engaged in their learning, which is why we need to rebrand assignments into memorable learning experiences. Moving away from question-and-answer classwork, we must establish rich projects that offer synthesis possibilities for students. In this way, they will learn to master skills and recognize their own growth as learners and collaborators. Consider what learning looks like in your space. How many truly memorable projects and experiences do kids have? How might grading these experiences diminish the possibilities? What do you need to do to truly rebrand assignments?

HACK 4

FACILITATE STUDENT PARTNERSHIPS

Work smarter, not harder

You can teach a student a lesson for a day; but if you can teach him to learn by creating curiosity, he will continue the learning process as long as he lives.
— CLAY P. BEDFORD, INDUSTRIALIST

THE PROBLEM: TEACHERS ARE IN CHARGE OF WHAT AND HOW STUDENTS LEARN

WHEN THERE IS only one person in the room capable of providing useful feedback, there is no way every child will get what he or she needs all of the time. When a teacher is the only one giving feedback, students miss opportunities for growth. Teaching what you know demonstrates a high level of mastery, one we hope that all students attain. If teachers maintain control of this element of learning, too many students miss out. Serious educational consequences result when teachers dominate the feedback loop.

- The imbalanced ratio of one teacher to many learners makes it challenging to meet all student needs.

- Limiting control by placing it solely in the hands of the teacher causes students to become dependent, rather than independent, learners.

- It is impossible to capitalize on all of the expertise in the room, and therefore valuable resources are wasted.

THE HACK: TEACH STUDENTS TO BE PEER REVIEWERS

Students want to be involved in the process—they just don't realize that they can be. By the time most students get to high school, they are so used to being told what is right and wrong that they don't know they are allowed to have an opinion. It's time we change this.

Teachers can invest class time for teaching students how to be feedback experts in specialized areas and excellent peer conference leaders. This process can take time, but the payoff is worth every second. Considering other peoples' work and giving guidance for improvement is challenging for everyone, including adults. So, we must support students until they feel confident in their ability to help others.

Having students champion each other's work benefits both the learner and the teacher. When students help others they become better, keener learners themselves, and the teacher is freed up to work with students who need more help than a peer can offer. Plus, student partnerships alleviate many of the time constraints that accompany project creation and ongoing assessment.

WHAT YOU CAN DO TOMORROW

The process of training students in this way can start tomorrow. Once a first draft or the beginning phases of a project are in the works, the teacher can set up stations to start training students.

Show students how it's done. Modeling the behaviors we expect is always essential, so show students what it means to provide meaningful feedback. For example, take a piece of work, highlight one specific element of it and then share what you observe in the work that meets assignment guidelines. It's always good to lead with positive feedback and then address an area that needs improvement. If you are giving feedback on a science lab, for example, you can say the lab efficiently restates the steps, but the conclusion does not yet fully explore the findings. Feedback will be different, depending on the student's age and the sophistication of the content. Regardless of what you teach, feedback should always be specific and offer strategies for improvement.

Divide students into groups of three or four to become experts in a particular area. Group students purposefully, in order to maximize their abilities. Consider mixed levels of learners to make the groups most useful. Anticipate any problems individuals may have when it comes to providing or receiving feedback.

Teach a mini-lesson in a particular area of expertise. Prepare a mini-lesson on the process of giving feedback and introduce the idea of expert groups to the students. Make sure they understand that they are all learning how to be experts and why a feedback loop is important. Give them time to reflect and ask questions about providing feedback to their peers; they will have plenty.

Teach students how to put comments on documents if they are using technology. Google Docs is a useful tool for this activity—students can share ideas in real time whether they use Macs or PCs. Add comments by highlighting text and either using the pull-down menu or *command* + *option* + M on a Mac or *command* + M on a PC. Remind students always to hit "comment" when they are done or the feedback won't save.

A BLUEPRINT FOR FULL IMPLEMENTATION

Step 1: Put students in their expert groups and let them get to know each other.

Before you can allow groups to set out on their own, group members must be acquainted with each other. Providing students time to work together will help them learn each member's learning style. Who will take the lead? What role will each person play? How will they collaborate? Roles can vary based on the content and task: A leader keeps the group on task, someone else keeps time, and the others will offer suggestions on how best to work together.

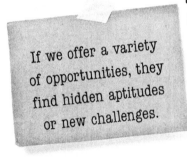

If we offer a variety of opportunities, they find hidden aptitudes or new challenges.

Step 2: Review how to use the technology.

Although feedback can be done on paper, it is much more efficient when using a platform like the Google Educational Suite. Google Docs allows for easy sharing and commenting. There are also many Chromebook extensions that may enhance the feedback process. No matter what platform you're using for feedback, it's important to review the process periodically; never assume students fully understand the technology.

Step 3: Work with individual groups to hone expertise in a particular area.

Once groups are established, you will want to work with them individually, walking them through the specific feedback area they will be using. Help them identify common challenges as a starting point and then develop a bank of good feedback phrases and strategies that will help guide other students.

Another good activity is to work with students to develop rubrics. This will help them understand success criteria and phrasing to use for specific feedback. As they put the feedback on the documents, they should make specific reference to the standards language that the rubric uses.

Step 4: Provide class time for students to work together to norm the feedback.

Students need ample time to practice in class so that they can work effectively at home. Allow students to work together in teams during class time so you can oversee their feedback at first and answer questions as they arise. Encourage them to ask questions if they are unsure, or even to question the person for whom they are providing the feedback. You'll want to strengthen the confidence of the student experts by giving specific praise for their efforts or helping them to readjust as quickly as possible to ensure they don't convey wrong information.

Step 5: Practice frequently.

This is the kind of activity that requires practice, so give students opportunities to offer feedback frequently over a period of time. It may not work completely the first few times you try it. Even more advanced learners will struggle early because providing legitimate feedback will be an unknown for most. Encourage students to continue the dialogue. Remind them of the value of their partnerships. Tell them that doubt is okay and that it's okay to miss things. Assure them that you'll have their backs. As the year progresses, all students will become better at assessing peers and themselves.

Step 6: Rotate groups to ensure many opportunities.

It's important to offer students opportunities to try out different roles in each area of expertise. Although we start students in one area, we must offer new challenges once they master particular roles during the process. Sometimes students won't know they have an aptitude for something until they try it. Often students learn too late that they can be good at many things because they've been given the chance to work only in one area. If we offer a variety of opportunities, they find hidden aptitudes or new challenges.

Step 7: Make peer feedback a class routine.

Routines solve many problems because students can rely on their consistency. When a routine or protocol is in place, students will learn to navigate the system and eventually they will not come to the teacher for every question. They learn to rely on each other, knowing that the teacher is there for emergencies and for those cases when other students can't help.

Step 8: Empower students to perpetuate the routine.

Almost more important than establishing the routine is allowing students to be in charge of it moving forward. Empower leaders in the class to be your "go to" students and support them as they help other students in the class. These learning opportunities will help them grow and allow for differentiation to happen organically.

Step 9: Adjust as needed.

With every plan there must be some adjustment, so be vigilant and make sure to fine-tune as needed. Continue to monitor the status of the class to ensure that routines are accomplishing the desired task. Make small adjustments with mini-lessons, small-group conversations, or one-on-one corrections. One great way to test if things are working is to check in with each student and follow up with a reflection exit ticket. Make sure students know that their voices are being heard. Consider asking, "How is it going? What problems are you experiencing?" A tool like Socrative makes this a painless task that provides amazing feed-back to teachers, while taking very little time.

OVERCOMING PUSHBACK

Understanding mindset will help you to see where some of the push-back originates. Many teachers are reluctant to give up control. They may have complaints, as will the students and parents. Here are a few examples and possibilities for dealing with the issues.

Students aren't qualified to provide feedback. True. At first, many teachers aren't qualified to provide expert feedback because they are stuck in the grades world. Like teachers, students are learning and practicing together, and expertise will take time. The more helpers we have in the room, the better the learning environment will be. We are leveraging the gifts that some students have naturally, enhancing them, and putting them to work so that every child gets what he or she needs. Students may not start out "qualified," but they do learn quickly.

My peers don't give feedback as well as the teacher. Students may complain that their peers don't do a good enough job or won't work outside of class. If this happens, you must talk to students and ensure that the work gets done. By providing class time, you can make sure that all students are doing their parts and doing them well. Some students' feedback may not be as effective as the teacher's or other peers' at first, but with more practice, they become proficient at specific skills. Remind students of the value of peer assessment, and explain that it is okay to struggle; it's part of the learning process. Tell them that your goal is for them to be as good as you at assessing how well students learn. They will love hearing this, and their confidence will grow.

Only teachers should be helping students. Some may say that teachers are the ones who get paid to do this job, so they shouldn't foist their responsibility on students. However, in the 21st century, teaching isn't limited to the teacher; this is an old way of thinking. Real learning happens while doing, so we must provide students every opportunity to take command of their learning. Learners move forward through a cycle of empowerment, practice, failure, and more practice. Think of how many learning opportunities we'd be stealing from kids if we kept all of this important work in the teacher's hands. Plus, teaching kids to provide feedback doesn't mean teachers are shirking their duties. In fact, most good educators will argue that teaching students to effectively discuss learning is a teacher's greatest responsibility.

This can only work in ELA classrooms. Allowing students to take the reins doesn't have to be the norm only in language arts classes; it can work for every content area. Let students be explorers and experts, freeing the teacher to facilitate specific differentiation as needed. A good first step in a math or science class might be teaching peer evaluators to ask, "Why did you do it this way?" or "If you try this, how does the solution change?" For creative-minded educators, student partnerships offer limitless paths to learning.

THE HACK IN ACTION

My journalism class runs an effective student media outlet, which would not be possible if the students were not empowered to be in charge. If our goal is to help students become responsible, independent thinkers and doers, we must trust the process and them.

In our newsroom, student leaders are in charge of everything. The editor-in-chief oversees it all. The section editors supervise their areas of expertise, the web team maintains the website, and the managers ensure that everyone is productive. They all report to me to let me know what is going on. Meanwhile, I work with struggling students who need help with the writing.

Once routines are established, which takes time and practice, student editorial leaders must be trained. The *WJPSnews.com* staff knows the necessity of good, balanced reporting and accurate writing for an audience. In the beginning, I had my hands in everything, which really stunted the learning process, but it was necessary to establish the routine. Once leaders were trained to give good feedback, answer questions, and use the technology, staff reporters became confident reporting to who was in charge, and it wasn't me.

An average day at *WJPSnews.com* probably looks like organized chaos. Students work on independent, self-paced, and self-chosen tasks to benefit the health of the newspaper. First they visit the Google Spreadsheet where we collaborate and inform each other on what is being reported. They select a topic (either one the teacher generates or one they generate themselves) and assign themselves a deadline, which is usually one week from the start date. If a topic isn't appropriate (although this happens infrequently), the editor from the section will flag it and confer with the reporter after checking with me.

From there, the students research, interview, and draft their articles in and out of class. They have access to laptops and their cell phones most every day, and they are allowed to leave the classroom with a press pass as needed. Once a draft is started, it is shared with the section editor and the teacher, who review it and provide feedback as appropriate within the timeline. First draft feedback is always about content. Are things clear? Does the writer answer all of the questions? Are there varied voices from the student body? We avoid correctness feedback on the first pass. That comes later at the copyediting level.

After content feedback, the reporter goes back to work, gathers more research and interviews, hyperlinks all necessary information and re-sends the document, ensuring that the editor's concerns have been answered. When the section editor deems the article complete, it is sent to fresh eyes with the editor-in-chief. If no further changes are necessary it travels to the fact checker, the copy editor, and finally to the web team for posting.

As the teacher, I oversee this process, but I'm not actively involved in it. I'm in the business of "putting out fires," always reminding students that a free and open press requires their responsibility and commitment. During class time, I circulate and check in with students, confer, or troubleshoot. The more control students have, the more time the teacher has to work with students who need specific help.

Because the class functions so well under student leadership, we have been able to sustain momentum from one year to the next. With my help, the current leaders train the next year's editors midway through the year. This sets the new students up for success, since they understand the responsibility and the amount of self-discipline that running a newspaper will entail. They see students in roles of power, and know that they must be as reliable if the paper is to continue operating effectively.

It's important to remember that school is about our students, not us, so the more we can empower them to be in control of their learning, the better. By making them partners in the feedback process we give them the valuable experience of helping and collaborating with others.

Consider who has the control of the feedback in your classroom. Where can students be more empowered to take control? What first steps could be put in place to begin a trusting partnership? How will your role change in this student-driven environment?

DIGITIZE YOUR DATA

Ease data collection and inform learning with technology

It is important to remember that educational software, like textbooks, is only one tool in the learning process. Neither can be a substitute for well-trained teachers, leadership, and parental involvement.

— KEITH KRUEGER, EDUCATION TECHNOLOGIST

THE PROBLEM: DATA COLLECTION

IN TODAY'S EDUCATION world, where "data" is the most frequently used buzzword, teachers are often charged with gathering information that in many cases is never used. Binders are collated and organized, clipboards are purchased, and dozens of spreadsheets are made, most with no further application.

Whether teachers are supposed to analyze testing data or generate classroom observational data, they rarely put it to use. There isn't enough time in the day to explore all of the data that gets collected because we are so busy gathering and analyzing it.

Explain why or why not you feel the group understands the concepts of satire, be specific *

Based on what you know about satire, what elements of the movie employs those techniques?

The Group effectively understood and used Great Expectations to create something creative *

Elements of the actual text were accurate and appropriate

Which of the following standards do you believe the group is meeting? *

Check all that apply

- R.1.2 Studfents comprehend elements of literary texts
- R2.2 Students use context to comprehend and elaborate the meaning of texts
- R3.2 Students interprets, analyzes and critiques author's use of literary and rhetorical devices, language and style
- W1.1 Students analyze components of purpose, goals, audience and genre
- W2.2 Students generates, selects, connects and organizes information and ideas
- W3.1 Students generate text to develop points within the preliminary organizational structure
- Students make stylistic choices with language to achieve intended effect
- W5.4 Students prepare text for presentation/publication
- S3.1 Students analyzes purpose, audience, and context when planning a presentation or performance
- S3.4 Students presents, monitors audience engagement and adapts delivery
- M1.1 Students understand teh nature of media communication
- M2.2 Students develop and produce a creative media communication
- students understand the technology and editing process

Figure 5.1

Here are just a few problems with traditional data collection:

- There is too much data collection without enough action

- Data collection methods are time-consuming

- The data collected doesn't enhance student learning

- Teachers gather data in isolation and often lose valuable opportunities to get to the heart of what is happening

THE HACK: DIGITIZE YOUR DATA FOR MORE EFFICIENT CLASSROOM LEARNING

There is a way to streamline the data collection process and then meaningfully use that data for learning. Using Google Forms or some other digital tool like it, teachers can include students in the assessment process and create a real-time result that is traceable, editable, and sharable.

Figure 5.1 is a snippet of a student form, created to generate feedback and data, after viewing student movies.

I share the information from this form with students, and we set goals based on the feedback. I am able to skip the usual data entry because the form collects the information and generates the spreadsheet, so sharing the information is much easier and more efficient. Including students this way provides more specific data that a teacher can use to adjust instruction.

WHAT YOU CAN DO TOMORROW

While this is an ongoing process, there are immediate steps you can take to begin digitizing your data:

Create a form and share it with students. Creating a form with a tool like Google Drive or SurveyMonkey is easy and takes only a few minutes. Start tomorrow by generating a short needs assessment or a quick "Where are you now?" form. This means literally posting one or two questions to your platform of choice, providing an answer space beneath the questions, clicking "Publish" and sharing a link to the form with students.

Take pictures of student learning. Instead of writing everything down, use your smart phone or tablet to take pictures or short video clips of student learning that you can review later or share with parents and a wider community. You may want to refer to "The Glass Classroom" section in *Hacking Education: 10 Quick Fixes for Every School* (the first *Hack Learning Series* book) for more information about backchanneling your classroom. There are many web tools and apps that provide excellent cloud-based storage space for student work samples and narrative feedback.

Create a class hashtag on Twitter. Build a conversation about learning with students in and out of class with a unique Twitter hashtag. My classes have their own hashtags—#WJPSnews for Newspaper and #WJPSAPlit for AP Literature. Make sure to use your school initials, in order to make your hashtag unique; this keeps unwanted participants out of the conversation. Be sure students understand how hashtags aggregate tweets into one easy-to-read stream. There are many brief YouTube videos that illustrate how to effectively use Twitter hashtags.

A BLUEPRINT FOR FULL IMPLEMENTATION

Step 1: Create a template that you can re-use and revise.

Once you have found a platform, it's time to start developing some templates that you can use with all of your classes for different kinds of data collection. Here are a few tips:

- Make the form generic, but include a question that allows the students to say which class they are in. This general query makes the form easily customizable. This will also help when cutting and pasting to create new forms.

- Make sure the form has a clear purpose. For example, if you're preparing for a conference, label it as such, and include goal setting and feedback collection. At the end of the term you may want a lengthier reflective form that can also serve as a scaffolding tool. Be cautious, though, because long forms tend to get clunky in the middle.

- Keep most forms short, something the students can fill out in a few minutes.

- Create a form to use as an exit ticket at the end of class.

- Consider creating forms describing growth around specific standards or skills.

- Always ask yourself, "What data do I need?" and ask students for the information that matches your needs.

Step 2: Review the data.

Take time to review the data, first on your own, and then with the students if you have questions. Add notes and feedback that help students establish goals and strategies, based on your findings.

Step 3: Adjust instruction based on the data.

Once you have reviewed the data, determine the best course of action. It's helpful to reflect and ask yourself some key questions:

- Does something need to be re-taught to the whole class, a small group, or one student? Are we ready to move to the next topic?

- Should anything be changed for future lessons?

- Are different activities around the same skills or concepts needed to provide students with opportunities to move toward mastery?

Step 4: Share the data with colleagues who teach the same students.

Conferring with colleagues can be challenging if a common meeting time isn't available. Sharing data electronically between team members is efficient, and if you use Google Forms, the spreadsheet will allow other users to add their own information, ask questions, and enter observations into the spreadsheet. This will save time when you do meet in person, as you will have already addressed many of the issues. This way, you may solve simpler challenges without having to meet face to face. The "Meet Me in the Cloud" section in *Hacking Education* may offer other helpful ideas about conferring in the cloud.

Step 5: Continue to update information as the year progresses.

To use data successfully, you will need to update information periodically. You don't need to update every student's file every day, but you should definitely add and adjust information over the course of an activity or unit. Always make sure to date the changes so your records remain accurate. If you've chosen a program that will work on your phone, updating becomes even easier.

Step 6: Back up and label your data.

Save your work regularly and use a title for the document that will be easy to locate later. You should also routinely back up information onto a flash drive in the event that a cloud-based service like Google isn't working.

OVERCOMING PUSHBACK

Technology can be a polarizing subject, as many people like to do things a familiar way even if they understand that it isn't the most effective way to do it. Here is some advice for dealing with folks who push back against digitizing the data:

Technology isn't always available. If you select a platform that also features a mobile app, you can work from your phone or tablet, making technology available at all times. Most cloud-based storage bins (Drive, Dropbox, Evernote, to name just a few) have free mobile applications, simplifying data collection for teachers and students. It's understandable that school Wi-Fi may be slow or down occasionally, but students can always add data from home or another location, like a library. Students will only need access to email to get into a form. In a worst-case scenario, students can also write out data you want to collect by hand and you can type it into the online form later.

I don't know how to use the technology. Not knowing how to do something can be scary, but it shouldn't stop education shareholders from moving forward. Turn to colleagues and administrators for help. Find a support team to help sift through the thousands of resources available online, as a mountain of tutorials can actually create a steeper learning curve for newbies. Remind parents and colleagues that taking a chance on new technology will have a huge impact on teaching and learning.

How is this any different than doing it by hand? Too often we write information in notebooks and never return to it, or we lose the notebook. Data collected online is conveniently organized and accessed from anywhere. It integrates smoothly into other places, and cutting and pasting makes it especially easy to copy student feedback into objectives and differentiation plans. Plus, today's learners prefer to work online, so they are more likely to add valuable information and respond to feedback that is stored in the cloud.

THE HACK IN ACTION

The first time I brought Google Forms into the classroom, my form was clunky and student response was thin. As with everything we do for the first time, I needed to carefully consider what my forms were trying to achieve and stop trying to do everything at once. So I revised the form and re-sent it to the students. I gave them class time to execute the survey in a meaningful way; this way if they had questions, I was available to answer them on the spot.

I walked around the classroom and read over their shoulders while they completed the survey at their own pace. Ideas about how to work with them were already beginning to bubble. I realized that some students didn't understand the topic as well as I thought they had. For example, when my ninth-grade ICT students responded to questions about journalism ethics, their answers showed me only a cursory understanding. We needed to spend more time on this, and I knew exactly how to help them grasp what they had missed.

Since the first pass was largely a reading activity, we needed to do something more hands-on. I made the second assignment a skit. As a group, they had to develop an ethical dilemma that journalists face and then walk us through how the journalist solved the problem. When I sent the same form back after the second assignment, all of the students had got it. In addition to learning that they needed more time, I learned that for this group of students, hands-on acting activities were more meaningful than reading alone. Once I collected this data, I could adjust the outcome on the spreadsheet that the form generated, and I was able to rethink what would happen next, predicated on what I had learned from the data.

With this particular set of students, I learned as the year progressed that giving them too many options was actually detrimental to their growth. Too many choices paralyzed them, and I doubt I would have learned this had I not offered them the chance to share their learning with me through this data collection process. Observation alone wasn't enough.

Toward the end of the year, I was able to go back through the data, revise the final evaluation for the year, and help students prepare for their self-evaluation forms. These activities all tied together nicely, and the students understood the benefits of working in the cloud.

This data collection method made my teaching process transparent. The forms helped me scaffold the expectations for later, when students moved away from answering directed questions to completing written reflections. Throughout the process students became more articulate when addressing their own needs, which helped me hone class time.

This is the kind of efficiency we must strive for to ensure growth for every child in our space, regardless of how big our classes are. Class size can no longer be used as an excuse not to collect and use data. We have a responsibility to every child in our care, so we must find methods to make the job of data collection manageable.

Data in education is never going to go away, so if we can find more efficient ways to gather and use it, then both our practice and our students improve. Consider your current data-gathering practices. What are you currently doing that can be improved? How can you use the data to push learning even further in your classes?

HACK 6

MAXIMIZE TIME

Confer inside and outside of class

Time is the most valuable thing a man can spend.
— THEOPHRASTUS, GREEK PHILOSOPHER

THE PROBLEM: THERE ARE TOO MANY STUDENTS
AND NOT ENOUGH TIME TO CONFER DURING CLASS

TIME IS ALWAYS at a premium in classrooms and in most schools classes are much larger than they should be. Meeting students' needs in these situations is extremely challenging and often students fall through the cracks. Despite our best efforts to make class time meaningful, most teachers struggle even to check in with students daily, so the idea of in-class conferring seems impossible.

- Class sizes are too big to personalize learning.

- Mandated curriculum seems to require teacher-centered teaching.

- Too much content to cover makes it impossible to take "time off" to work with students independently.

- There isn't enough time during a normal class period.

THE HACK: MAXIMIZE TIME

How we spend our time in class is indicative of what we prioritize in education, so if we want to meet student needs, we must learn to use class time more. There are ways to prepare students for in-class conferences that can leverage the limited time we share. Time is better spent when we ask students to complete conference forms that we create to help them organize their ideas before they meet with us.

The teacher must be organized too. Having information from the students before you sit with them increases the flow and efficiency of class time. Generating a schedule and collecting data also helps. When class time isn't enough, remember that technology is also useful as a support. Use the devices that are available to you and the students to continue the conversation outside of class.

WHAT YOU CAN DO TOMORROW

Once we realize that students can have their needs met and teachers can maximize the use of shared class time, there is nothing holding us back.

Download an app like Voxer. Ask your students to do the same. Voice apps or walkie-talkie apps will allow you to have a conversation that extends over a period of time when people can't meet in person, and these tools have functions that help facilitate ongoing dialogue, while enhancing communication skills. Best of all, an app like Voxer can be used with any age child. For elementary students, the teacher can share a message or ask a question and individuals can reply by recording feedback on the notes feature, contained in the teacher's account. Alternatively, most smart phones and tablets have built-in voice recording applications, which may suffice for recording feedback from younger students.

 Create a short form to enhance conversation. To help students prepare for in-class conferences, you will want them to be thinking about something specific before they are in front of you. Give them questions to answer that will help focus the three to five minutes you have together.

 Make a schedule. Being organized will be essential to helping the class flow during classroom conferences. If students know the time of their conferences and can be prepared for them, conferences will move along efficiently.

 Use your student experts to help streamline issues in class. Since students are already trained as experts, empower those leaders to take the status of the class on a piece of paper and report back at the end of class. It may help to maintain a notebook with all of the data for future reference.

 Implement project time during conferences. If students are working on a project, you won't have to be in front of the room or circulate when it comes time for conferences. Whether students are working in groups or independently, they need to be engaged in some activity, so they do not interfere with your individual assessment conferences.

A BLUEPRINT FOR FULL IMPLEMENTATION

Step 1: Prepare for conferences by reviewing student feedback before meeting with individuals.

Since you have asked students to fill out the form in advance, take the time to read what they wrote so that you can maximize the conference. Asking them to set goals or establish what they are interested in talking about will give you a chance to prepare and avoid resorting to your own agenda. At the minimum, make sure to read the student's notes on the day of the conference.

Step 2: Instruct students to write specific questions they want answered during assessment conferences.

In addition to responses to the pre-assessment form, students should arrive at assessment conferences with specific questions about their progress. This will help in their reflection process and keep the discussion focused on each individual's progress and goals. You'll be less likely to waste time talking about issues unrelated to learning when a student is well prepared.

Step 3: Set conferences for 3-5 minutes and adhere to the schedule.

Maintaining a schedule is the key to keeping your conferences flowing smoothly. Have a hard copy of the schedule for the week on your desk at all times. Although flexibility will be necessary in the event of absent or unprepared students, the closer you stick to the plan, the more efficient your conferences will be.

Step 4: Follow up with students electronically.

Develop a strategy to follow up with students within a week of the conference. You'll want to make sure that students are working as planned or see if there is any additional troubleshooting that needs to be done. Having technology that you and the students agree on improves this process. You can easily message students on Voxer, Google Drive, or another application, from outside of class at your leisure. Fill down time (sitting in a doctor's waiting room, for example) with quick digital messages to students, continuing the conversation about learning.

Step 5: If more time is needed, plan a conference outside of class time.

Some students will require more time than you can provide in class and that's okay—just make sure to set time aside. Personally, I like to meet before school starts for 10-15 minutes where possible; otherwise, we make a lunch meeting. If your school sets aside time for extra help, students may prefer to come then or after school. Sometimes it's hard to accommodate busy students; this is where technology can be useful—have a virtual conference. Today's digital natives love communicating virtually.

Step 6: Teach students to use technology to get their questions answered.

With social media, other students can be resources even when they are not physically present. If you have a class Twitter hashtag, students can answer their peers' questions there. They can also add resources that can later be curated in a different online space to help everyone. For example, if one of my students is having a challenge with writing introductory paragraphs, I might post a link to the class hashtag that provides additional tips. Other students and teachers on Twitter can provide help too. Students might open the linked website or document and save it to a separate application, like Diigo—a web-based bookmarking tool and digital archive. When students review archived content, they might return to Voxer, Twitter, or a class website and ask a follow-up question. This is one more way teachers continue the conversation while maximizing time.

Step 7: Employ a routine or protocol that will keep work moving forward.

As with almost anything in education, routines facilitate success. The first time you try to do in-class conferences they may not go as planned, but this doesn't mean the process is a failure. Consider your mistakes, which may involve the structure of your form, pre-conference questions, your attitude toward particular students, the class environment, or other factors, and adjust as needed for future conferences.

Consider using different kinds of conferences throughout a term, but always meet with every child in formal, prepared meetings at least twice. In high school, I like to meet with students at midterm before progress reports and at the end of the term before the report card grades are due since they will be working with me to establish those grades. Small-group meetings are useful during collaborative projects. Individual conferences could be available during set office hours, or by appointment to fit in with your own schedule.

OVERCOMING PUSHBACK

Since time is at a premium in class, teachers are always reluctant to change the way class time runs. Also, many teachers have a hard time giving up enough control to allow students to work independently, which is required for this method to work. Here are some tips for some common challenges you might face when implementing class conferences with students:

There are too many students in this class for this to work. Assessment conferences can work even in large classes, but it requires having a protocol in place so the other students know what they are doing while the teacher is conferring with students. It also requires a schedule. It may be impossible to get to every student in one or two days, depending on the size of the class, so setting aside about a week's time may be useful. It may also be a good idea to give students with higher needs appointments outside of class or use technology to ease the flow.

Regardless of the size of your class, every child will want a turn having the teacher's undivided attention, so it is important to remind students that when you're with someone, you aren't to be interrupted. The time is special to that person and should be sacrosanct unless there is an emergency.

What will the other students do while I'm working with one student? When classrooms are student-centered and project-based, students are accustomed to working independently—they don't need the teacher in front of the room to function effectively. If we encourage this kind of environment consistently, the way the teacher spends his or her time in class won't be an issue. Just be sure to prompt students prior to meetings that they must be prepared to work independently or collaboratively in a quiet setting, during assessment conferences.

What could possibly be achieved in 3-5 minutes with each child? If students are well prepared for the conferences, it's certainly possible to address specific challenges. If we stick to the prepared topics and avoid generalizations about the student's work or the class learning, it's surprising how much can be accomplished in a relatively short span of time. To ensure the time is used most effectively, work first with students who have come prepared. Address students with different challenges later. They will likely require more time; these are cases where continuing the conversation in the cloud may be necessary.

THE HACK IN ACTION

Garnet Hillman, former high school Spanish teacher, shares her story of successful classroom conferences.

> Throughout fifteen years as a high school Spanish teacher, my classroom transformed from a traditional setting and practice to a student-centered, learning-focused environment. This culture shift not only supported student growth and achievement, but also fostered significant gains once changes were in place. Assessment practice as an entity separate from instruction was revised to a process that was infused seamlessly into class on a daily basis. Fluidity in assessment and feedback allowed my students to learn at the highest levels, yet at their own pace to honor that natural learning process.
>
> Student conferences were a cornerstone in assessing my students. To me, the most powerful feedback for students derives from conversation. Meaningful dialogue provides a clear path forward while concurrently giving the instructor valuable insight on the learning progression for each student. Conferring gives students the ability to move forward

immediately, while other methods of feedback may take a little longer to be processed and internalized to advance.

In my classroom, conferences with students happened both informally and formally. I regularly made a concerted effort to talk with all of my students (although with 150 students I couldn't get to each one every day!). My students worked at their own pace, charting a course through language learning with me in the role of facilitator. Daily journaling led to efficient and effective conversations.

Rather than spending my time lecturing to the whole group, I frequently worked with small groups of students and met with individuals. Chatting with them throughout the class periods elicited better results than I had previously seen. I spoke with them about their ongoing work, asking more questions than giving strong directives. Students owned their learning and mapped out varied journeys. When the kids owned the process, engagement rose. When they knew the instructor was on their side, supporting them every step of the way, hope blossomed and success was on the horizon.

Formal conferring happened at the end of each marking period. Students had an individual time slot allotted for them to sit down with me and have a conversation. Although it took two to three days for this process, it was well worth the time. To assist with flow, productivity, and efficiency, students completed a written reflection prior to the conference. Topics for discussion included achievement, strengths, areas for growth, and goal setting. I made sure to ask the students about a moment when they felt proud in class. The impact of this question was significant. Students can be very hard on themselves and this granted an opportunity to reflect on a positive, inspirational moment.

In my current role as an instructional coach, I support teachers in the implementation of student conferences. They realize the powerful and successful outcomes far outweigh the class time spent in dialogue. Students are engaged, involved, and take leadership roles in their classes. A collaborative environment forms and students don't feel uneasy about the word "assessment." They are simply accustomed to how class runs and seek out meaningful conversations with instructors and classmates to further their learning.

With daily informal conversations and formal conferences, assessment and feedback loops naturally develop. These loops continually support students and bolster their confidence with regard to their progress and achievement. They become increasingly more proficient to self-monitor and provide peer assessment and feedback.

The most compelling outcome of student conferences is the relationships that form with students. Relationships unlock the door to student learning. I had many students tell me that they didn't love Spanish (of course some of them did), but they loved my class. They enjoyed the environment because they knew I cared about their learning and more important, about them as individuals. If I hadn't spent so much time talking with them, this would not have been possible.

The relationships would have been at a surface level and insubstantial. With these connections in place, self-advocacy skyrocketed. Students understood this environment was a safe place to ask questions, take risks, and create meaningful goals. Achievement levels soared—we celebrated success and built upon it. Looking forward, I hope to help more teachers see the cogent effect of student conferencing on learning.

We can all agree on the value of conferring with students regularly, but many of us struggle with balancing the time and needs of our many students while we do it. In order to truly make the no-grades classroom possible, conferences must become as important as other non-negotiables. Consider how you provide feedback to students now. How often do you meet with them one-on-one to talk about their growth and progress? Where would it make sense to fit more of it in?

HACK 7

TRACK PROGRESS TRANSPARENTLY

Discard your traditional grade book

To follow imperfect, uncertain, or corrupted traditions,
in order to avoid erring in our own judgment, is
but to exchange one danger for another.
— RICHARD WHATELY, ENGLISH ECONOMIST

THE PROBLEM: USING THE TRADITIONAL GRADE BOOK TO TRACK LEARNING

TRACKING LEARNING THE usual way won't work if you throw out grades: What would you write in the grade book? What grade books do is provide a space to write down letters and numbers, both arbitrary and useless, and by the time they are averaged for the report card, they are outdated and meaningless.

- Averaging grades diminishes student learning to one number.

- Traditionally, the teacher does all of the tracking privately.

- Students only have access to their progress a few times a year when report cards are issued.

- There isn't adequate space in a grade book to write down important anecdotal information.

THE HACK: TRACK STUDENT PROGRESS TRANSPARENTLY

By changing the way we track progress, we re-emphasize the partnership of learning between students and teachers. If we truly want to empower our students to be in charge of their own growth, then keeping notes about progress tucked away in a grade book that only a teacher sees seems counterproductive. There are many different ways to encourage tracking progress, but starting simply is usually the best way.

In a notebook, Google document, or spreadsheet, whichever the student prefers, ask students to generate a chart of four columns:

Assignment	Feedback	Standards Addressed	Strategy

Column headers may vary depending on what you want your students to track, but this is a good start. Put students in charge of recording the feedback they receive. This may be written or verbal feedback that has been communicated one-on-one or in a small group. It will take time to establish a routine, but one way to help students is to allow them to record verbal feedback on their phones or take pictures of written feedback so it is stored for future reference.

Your old grade book is a waste of space and time. Don't hesitate; just throw it out.

Eventually, students will be tracking all of the feedback they receive in class. When we put the power in their hands to record and remember, to work and improve, we relinquish the responsibility of tracking what every child needs all the time. This saves time and energy the teacher needs to help all students, and the person who most needs to know about a student's progress—the student—does know. Students can keep the teacher informed as they progress.

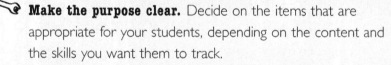

WHAT YOU CAN DO TOMORROW

Throw out your paper grade book. There is no need to keep it if students are taking on the responsibility for record keeping. As a matter of fact, your old grade book is a waste of space and time. Don't hesitate; just throw it out.

Make the purpose clear. Decide on the items that are appropriate for your students, depending on the content and the skills you want them to track.

Determine the best record-keeping method for your class—with or without technology. Every learning environment is different, so you must select what will work best for you and your class, based on students' ages, mastery levels, and access to technology.

Conduct a test run. No matter what point it is in your school year, it's important to immediately begin to develop a transparent system of tracking progress and feedback, even if it's only a test run. Although it will be easier to completely over-haul record keeping in August or September, you can begin adapting your system in January or even after spring break. Limit the risk by experimenting with one unit and call it a "beta test," in order to help "sell" it to students, parents, and administration.

A BLUEPRINT FOR FULL IMPLEMENTATION

It will take time to let go of the old and find the right system for your students. You may find that different students require different tracking methods, and as time goes on adjustment will be necessary. Exercise flexibility as you go.

Step 1: Generate two to three methods to share with your students to track their learning.

Create basic models to share with students based on their needs and the specifications of the unit. For example, if students are working on the scientific method, you'd want to have a different format for gathering feedback than if you were talking about solving math equations. Perhaps you have different T-charts or double-entry journal headings you want to use or maybe your visual learners need to track progress in a Venn diagram. Rather than letting them generate their own tracking methods at first, you may want to provide a selection of graphic organizers. As they become more proficient, encourage students to adjust their methods. This will be easier than allowing every child to create one of his or her own right away.

Step 2: Invite students to try a variety of methods to see which works best.

The first organizer may not work as well as the students or the teacher would like. Allow students the freedom to use a trial and error approach to finding the best tracking method. Since every child will have different needs, it's a good idea to let each of them decide which method is the best fit. You may want to put students with similar needs in pairs or threes at first. Then they will be able to work together the same way they do with peer feedback.

Step 3: Check in with students to ensure they are using effective learning strategies.

It's not enough to give students learning tools—teachers must follow up to see that the tools are being used. Put a procedure in place to ensure that students are using the learning strategies discussed in the feedback and adjusting them as needed. It's a good idea to have students explain how they are implementing suggestions from the feedback when they write reflections about their process (see Hack 8). This way the teacher will be able to follow up with more specific feedback regarding how well the strategies are working.

Step 4: Teach students to set goals based on feedback.

After students receive feedback and track it, they should set new goals based on their progress. Using strategies the teacher provides and the specific standards that the work addresses, students should set a manageable number of goals (three to five) that can be tracked through the next assignment. Short-term goals work best for student tracking; the collection of shorter goals will establish a pattern and show growth for the year.

Step 5: Use the goals to establish appropriate strategies with students.

Based on the new goals, adjust the strategies appropriately, according to student need. What kinds of strategies have worked before? Can they be adjusted and re-used in this particular situation? Do new ones need to be employed?

Perhaps you taught students how to highlight and annotate their writing as a revision technique and it was successful. You might use the same strategy for a new challenge that addresses a different standard. Or maybe you abandon the highlighters and move to sticky notes, or introduce ways to pose questions in marginal annotations for the new challenge. Whatever the issue, the new goals should dictate the strategies.

Step 6: As goals are reached, teach students to develop new ones.

Since students are tracking their own progress, there should be a formal way of acknowledging success once a student reaches a goal. Then it's time to develop a new goal based on the student's current needs. Have students record when they achieved each goal using a checkmark or a date and write down the evidence that shows how they knew it was achieved so it is accessible later. From there, students can consider where they need more growth. If a student needs help with this step, it's a good time for a conference to look at the work together.

OVERCOMING PUSHBACK

Students, in many cases, will be reluctant to take on more responsibility. Here are some issues people may raise and how to confront them.

If students can see their progress online, they will hyper-focus on feedback. While students have access to their learning progress via the online communication system, it doesn't have to become the focal point of daily learning. The same students who would have been hyper-focused on grades may want to rush the process of improvement, but you'll just need to have an open dialogue with these students about moving forward from wherever they are now.

Parents will have too many questions. Knowing this means we must be prepared with reasonable responses. Stick to the facts when talking to parents and use the work as talking points, but don't allow parental bullying to force you to change your practice. Depending on the district you work in and the level of parent involvement, some parents may be used to getting their way. They may even go above your head and try to get administration to strong-arm you into changing your practice. Administrators who understand the shift will support you and should back you in these situations. Make sure there is a plan in place in case the situation escalates.

Administration will expect all teachers to do this. Why wouldn't administration want all teachers to do something that is working for students? Some teachers may not want to change old practices because they are comfortable, but that doesn't mean their way is the best way. Administrators should broach the suggestion to change when teachers have a sufficient amount of time to get used to the new system. They should provide training to ease anxiety about the change in the technology so fewer teachers will be uneasy about changing their practice.

THE HACK IN ACTION

The way we track learning should suit the students and the teacher. Here is one example of how high school teacher Adam Jones tracks student progress.

> Teaching is an art form. It is a delightful dance of perspective-taking and feedback.
>
> Paradoxically, the most impactful teaching is often invisible to the learner. The teacher exists in the background to listen attentively and offer feedback when necessary. When this is done effectively, students learn how to learn. Increasingly complex adaptive challenges help develop learner curiosity, passion and efficacy. As a teacher, you've succeeded when you walk into the classroom and you know the students no longer need you. Independence has to be the supreme goal.
>
> The path to this end is rarely straight. It is a dance with each student to understand the starting point and investigate the role of feedback in the learning process. And that is why teaching is so dynamic, fluid, and fun. It is a chance to co-create a beautiful piece of art that, ultimately, the learner owns.
>
> I love being a learner. Consistently exercising those muscles feels really important when taking the perspective of

my students. I am in touch with what it means to be taught, and therefore I understand what I need to unlock my intrinsic motivation. For example, time to explore, examples to examine, opportunities to practice/fail, and access to the feedback of experts. Unsurprisingly, when I design a new class I am primarily focused on the perspective of the learner. These questions routinely come to mind:

- Would I be able to learn in this class?

- Would I be challenged, held accountable and discover a sense of ownership?

- What form(s) of ongoing feedback would most support my skill development?

- How could I effectively demonstrate that I've grown and developed a critical eye for the places I still need to grow?

Designing a class that adequately answers these questions and encourages learning is challenging. Never mind the more difficult challenge of actually tracking and making that learning visible. Detailed below is a description of what I've discovered are essential components of a class that encourages curiosity, passion and efficacy.

Accountability

In recent years, I have moved away from assigning numerical grades to my students' work. Instead we focus on levels of proficiency (no information, advancing toward the goal, meeting goal, excelling past goal) when talking about their demonstration of learning. In addition to the marker of proficiency comes consistent and copious amounts of feedback. A numerical grade or a description of one's level of proficiency means next to nothing without explanatory feedback.

At the start of the term, I create a master Google Spreadsheet that lists all of our assignments on the horizontal axis and our learning goals (Reading, Writing, Speaking, and Listening) and their subcategories on the vertical axis. Students make a copy of the document, share it with me, and we work together throughout the term to track their progress. Despite the simplicity of this system, it has assisted in keeping everyone aimed in the correct direction.

Additionally, students create Google Drive Digital Portfolios and share the folder with me. This cloud-based home serves as the visible headquarters for all their work—draft and final. I am eager to explore more integrated evidence-based learning information and tracking systems such as Chalkup and FreshGrade this year.

Feedback

Learning is all about feedback. Aside from setting the structure and expectations of the class, the most leverage for growth a teacher can consistently offer a learner is feedback. All assignments are opportunities to practice, receive feedback, and refine. I use the audio messaging app Voxer to maintain an open line of verbal feedback throughout the term. Whether I am providing verbal feedback on their speaking skills after a class-led discussion or summarizing, with particular emphasis, the narrative comments left on one of their Google Doc drafts, Voxer is an invaluable tool for personalization and relationship building.

I utilize the text messaging app Remind to send general announcements and after-class public praise to highlight examples of student learning. I regularly jump at the opportunity to use the formative assessment tools Socrative and Kahoot, to check for understanding, provide feedback, and course correct. Additionally, all students in my class create content to be published on their blog which has the potential to provide an authentic audience ready to offer feedback in the comments section.

Self-Reflection

It is an essential component of enduring learning that students revisit their work and communicate insights from their progress. Creating scaffolding for students to experiment with this type of meta-thinking is critical for them to understand where they started, where they are presently, and what work is left to complete to reach their learning goals.

Students in my class complete a weekly (exit ticket) self-reflection Google Form. The information from this form serves as the mind-jogging catalyst for the midterm and end-of-term reflection interviews with me. These recorded conversations last between 10-20 minutes per student and typically take two days of class time. Additionally, I have been experimenting with the screencasting app Explain Everything as a self-reflection tool as an alternative to the more narrative approach with Google Forms.

The starting point for effective class design and teaching is one's capacity to take the perspective of the learner and skillfully offer feedback. Further, if a transparent system of accountability is established; feedback is consistent, copious, and varied; and students develop a critical self-reflective eye, all the ingredients are present for learner independence to develop by way of curiosity, passion, and efficacy.

As we put kids in charge of their own learning, it is essential to remember that transparency is key. Teachers should no longer track the progress of students in isolation, adding marks for arbitrary things or recording homework completion. Nothing important fits in a grade book, so discard the grade book. Consider how you currently use your grade book and what might work more efficiently. Get kids involved in this process too; partner up to track the goals and progress of every child. Ask, "What can I do to make learning transparent?"

HACK 8

TEACH REFLECTION

Help students become better learners with metacognition

It takes courage...to endure the sharp pains of self-discovery rather than choose to take the dull pain of unconsciousness that would last the rest of our lives.
— MARIANNE WILLIAMSON, AUTHOR

THE PROBLEM: STUDENTS DON'T KNOW WHAT THEY'VE ACCOMPLISHED

EVEN THOUGH GRADES are commonly used to communicate learning, at times students still don't understand why they receive the grades they do. Some believe that the test scores or report card grades aren't representative of what they actually know because they haven't had ample time to display their growth. In most cases, students fail to grasp the specifics of their knowledge and skill set.

Since assessing learning has traditionally been the responsibility of the educator, students aren't always clear on the criteria for mastery. They don't know what level of proficiency they've achieved because they haven't been provided with specific information about what they've done well and what needs continued effort.

- Students are notoriously left out of the assessment process.

- Despite getting test scores or comments on projects, kids don't always know why they earned the grade they did.

- Students are often left without a voice in the process of learning.

- What students know isn't always communicated accurately in a final project alone.

THE HACK: TEACH STUDENTS TO REFLECT ON THE PROCESS OF LEARNING

When students learn to reflect meaningfully about their learning, they can participate in a dialogue with the teacher that allows them to work together to determine the actual level of mastery. No longer working in isolation, the teacher can now adequately discuss depth of learning, thereby helping students to communicate particular knowledge that is too often absent from their final products. After students provide the teacher with thorough information about their process, the teacher is in a better position to assess student learning.

Ask students to consider the following:

- What was my understanding of the task in my own words?

- What did I do to achieve success on the task?

- What challenges did I face and how did I overcome them?

- Which standards did I meet and what evidence from my work supports that assessment?

- What goals did I set and meet? Which do I still need to work on?

- If I had the opportunity to do it again, what would I do differently?

A way of providing excellent feedback is to read the student's reflection and review the data you collected while the student was working before you assess the work. The teacher will have a clearer idea of what he or she is looking at, and will thus be able to provide every child with accurate individualized feedback.

In short, teachers cannot look at all student work the same way because every student starts in a different place. To ensure maximum progress to mastery we need to give every child feedback tailored to his or her specific needs.

Self-reflection also resolves the challenge of assessing group work. When every child presents a personal reflection, the teacher has a much better idea of what each child gained from working in the group. Consider what role the child played and how he or she grew. Remind students not to complain about other group members in their reflections, as the reflections should illustrate their own work, not their peers' work. Each student therefore receives fair assessment on the merits of his or her work and growth during the group project. In addition, the whole group should receive feedback on the project, focusing on how well they were able to meet standards. You can do this with a group email or short conference.

WHAT YOU CAN DO TOMORROW

Teaching students to reflect takes time, but it's well worth the commitment. There are things you can do right away to prime the learning:

Find out what they already know about reflection. Ask students what their understanding of reflection is by engaging in a conversation about it. Have they done it before? What does it look like? What should it include?

🗝 **Co-construct a list of items to be included in a reflection.** Take time in class to do a brainstorm with students, allowing them to contribute to the checklist.

🗝 **Show them an example of a reflection that exhibits mastery.** Nothing works better than showing a child what the expectation is, so allow students to read a good reflection and discuss what they notice with their groups. (See the sample in Hack 1.)

🗝 **Ask students to reflect at the end of class.** To get students into the habit of reflecting—and it is a habit that requires practice—ask them to consider what they have learned at the end of every class. This will also facilitate writing across content areas.

A BLUEPRINT FOR FULL IMPLEMENTATION

Step 1: Plan a lesson that shows students what reflection is.

Gather a few samples of good evidence-based reflections. Put students into groups and ask them to read and compare the reflections. What do they notice? How do the reflections compare? Ask them to generate a list of things they learned about reflections. In a full-class discussion, have students share why reflection can help their learning.

Step 2: Have students make a poster for the classroom that inspires reflection.

Once students grasp what reflection is about, have them synthesize what they've learned to present as a visual reminder for the class. Encourage them to consider these inquiries:

- What essential questions must be answered in a reflection?

- How can a student use reflection at the end of an assignment to communicate learning?

Hang the posters on the wall as an important resource throughout the year.

Students will see their own work and words about reflection and have a renewed understanding of why they are doing it. Share posters with colleagues so that all students are receiving a similar message.

Step 3: Teach the standards and skills.

If reflection is to be effective, students must understand the standards they aim to master. Help students understand why they are working on specific projects:

- What are they supposed to be learning?

- How do these skills align with content and standards?

- How does the work connect with other learning?

Devote class time to reviewing the standards that apply to each project/assignment/unit before you get started and then refer to them throughout. Make sure students have internalized the expectations and are able to talk about them in their own terms.

Step 4: Make reflection routine.

Reflection is most effective when it happens regularly. As with any skill, constant practice will improve the process and generate deeper understanding. Students should reflect during the last five minutes of class: Just ask them to write about something they learned and something they need to work on. Students should specify their goals and the strategies they used and present evidence from their work. They can also connect topics to what's being studied in different classes.

Step 5: Provide feedback on reflections regularly.

If we want students to improve the quality of reflection, we need to give them specific, immediate feedback when they reflect. Keep explanations simple:

- "You have provided an effective summary of the task, but you need to share more evidence of understanding."

- "This reflection does not discuss any standards."

- "Focus your reflection on your role in the group assignment and not on the work or lack of work of others."

- "Expand your discussion in this area to talk about what you learned or what you would do differently."

As students improve, make sure to acknowledge that you have noticed. Tell them you see specific improvement: "I noticed that you used standards this time with more evidence from your own work. Please make this a habit."

OVERCOMING PUSHBACK

Students will not like reflection at first; they will see it as additional work that doesn't feel like it's helping. Like most new things, students won't appreciate it until they see the growth later on. Be prepared for various complaints.

Why do I need to do this? Because reflection is the most important part of learning. Remind students that seeing how they reflect helps you provide useful feedback that will help them grow as learners. You'll need to exhibit the same patience you used when you convinced them to shift their mindsets.

This might be good for English but will it work for other subjects? Yes, reflection is valuable in English class, but it is also necessary in every other subject. I can't think of a subject area where students would not benefit from thinking about their learning, writing down what they have learned, and showing how they know that they learned it. Even more valuable is having students express what they struggle with and ask for the kind of help they'd like to receive to make it better. I'm sure a math student could talk about growth in proofs or challenges in trigonometry. Physical education students can reflect on their progress mastering lay-ups in basketball or on the challenges in maintaining a fitness regime. It is this reflection that encourages learners to set goals for improvement. Content should not dictate whether or not students reflect.

THE HACK IN ACTION

Once you convince students that you expect reflection and provide time for them to practice, reflection will increase learning. A perfect example is how math teacher Jim Cordery uses reflection with his students. Cordery emphasizes the power of reflection in his class.

> I have always tried to get my students to think differently about math, encouraging them to spend time thinking of their method to solving the problem over getting the actual answer. I spend time—my students probably think too much time—asking them to share their thinking behind their answers. To me, what is most important is that they are thinking about math.
>
> Over the last few years, I have thought about how I can increase participation in my classroom. Without a doubt, the addition of student reflections has been the answer I was looking for. I started including these reflections on every project and activity we completed. These are the benefits that resulted from giving my students a chance to reflect on a project or activity:

1. It makes them think about how the activity connects to the real world.

2. Reflecting has allowed me to communicate with everyone in class, not just the outspoken students.

3. I have them writing about how they are learning, not just finding an answer.

4. Reflection turns struggles into learning opportunities because I ask students to elaborate on what they struggled with.

5. They think about how the activity's objective could be used in their future profession or job.

6. I also get a chance to modify the activity for future use after analyzing my students' views on what they just completed.

Getting the students through this part of the journey is a challenge. I am constantly battling the phrase: "But this is math class. Why do we need to write?" I have attempted to counter this by initiating a conversation with my students. During this conversation, we discuss what is expected in the reflection. I point out that I am very interested in hearing about the process, but I am more interested in them sharing what struggles they overcame, both personally and as a group. I have taken the time to show past students' work (with names removed) where we discuss the pros and cons of each piece of work. I am conscious never to interject too much of my own reactions to the writing, because experience has shown I just get carbon copies of that exact piece.

Here is one example of a student's reflection:

Out of all of the projects and classwork papers I have completed throughout the school year, this project seemed to stand out. The project consisted of picking 5 destinations (cities) in the U.S that you wanted to visit; however, those cities also had to intertwine with U.S. history. After you have chosen your preferred destinations, you have to figure out how many miles it would take to go round trip. Starting and finishing at Philadelphia, the stops I made along the way included: Austin, Texas; Santa Fe, New Mexico; Los Angeles, California; Portland, Oregon; and Charleston, South Carolina. This trip was a sightseeing trip and like you would in a realistic situation, you had to figure out how much it would cost to eat, stay at the hotels, fuel your car, and rent a car.

This entire project was at each individual's pace, which worked out extremely well for me. I can go as fast as I wanted without having to wait, while I also could take time on specific parts of the project I might have been confused about. While this project tied in with U.S. history, it not only taught me pre-algebra, math, and setting proportions, it also included a life lesson that I will know for a lifetime. Time management and being wise with your money are crucial understandings that I will need to know in the future. For example, I didn't want my trip to be year-long, and I also didn't want to pick the Jeep (the most expensive car available to drive my 7,650 mile journey) because it was a cool car.

The math needed to finish this project is tedious and hard. The fact that this project had multiple steps really encouraged me to try and get one step done each day and to strive for two. The pleasure I received during this project was from part 2. In this section you had to figure out how many miles per gallon your car could go. The reason why is because I feel as if I worked the hardest on this part over all of the others. The math needed to complete this portion was meticulous and I was intrigued even more each car I completed. Before the completion of this project, I was forced to face rough patches along the way. The hardest part might seem silly to you; nevertheless, it was pretty difficult for me. Sometimes choices are good and they allow you to do what you want; however, a bit more boundaries might have helped me finish this task a bit faster. Being able to pick your own cities was actually the hardest part for me because I am not very quick at picking choices. With over thousands and thousands of cities all over the United States, to only pick five was a bit arduous.

Overall, this project broadened my horizons and helped me learn about math, social studies, and daily life situations. To be able to do projects similar to this one would be great because I really enjoyed everything involved with it. From the Civil War to the Battle of Fort Sumter, the cities I chose tied in perfectly with U.S. history, while they also were cities that I would want to visit in real life.

The traditional structure of education doesn't really allow for formal written reflection. We must spend time teaching students to think about their learning and the process they completed to get there. As students become better at reflection, they will be better able to ask for specific help to move forward. This gift can't be underestimated. Consider if or when you take time to teach kids to think about their processes. When would reflection be appropriate in your classes? How might this process support work you're already doing?

HACK 9

TEACH STUDENTS TO SELF-GRADE

Put the power of grading into students' hands

Life will never be close enough to perfect, and listening
to that voice means stepping outside of yourself and
considering your own wrongdoings and flaws.
— ASHLY LORENZANA, AUTHOR

THE PROBLEM: GRADES ARE SUBJECTIVE

WHEN A GRADE is calculated by averaging tests, projects, home-work, and class participation, the teacher often has only a cursory understanding of a student's actual learning. Even if the teacher has observed the student at work, what he or she sees is only part of the picture. Many times teachers think they know what students know and can do, but misjudge the reality. If we don't include students in the evaluation process, we are missing a vital piece of the puzzle.

Too often a teacher's bias plays a role in how students are graded. This prejudice is human, but unjust. For example, how many times has a student's reputation distorted your impression, even before you met him or her? Does a student's behavior change the way you read his or her work? Aren't there some kids you just like more than others, even though you'd never admit it?

- What teachers see is not always the full picture.

- Grades can be affected by prejudice.

- Leaving students out of the grading process denies students the right to show what they truly know and can do.

THE HACK: TEACH STUDENTS TO SELF-GRADE

Since traditional grades misrepresent learning, it is essential to teach students how to self-evaluate based on a set of standards or class expectations. We must give them the ability to look objectively at their bodies of work and determine their own levels of mastery by using evidence from their learning.

WHAT YOU CAN DO TOMORROW

Teaching students to self-evaluate will take time but that doesn't mean you can't get things started now. Here are some things you can do right away:

Stop grading student work without student input. What you see on the page and what is in a student's head may be different, so there is a better way. I understand that logistically it may be easier to grade alone at times, but we must bear in mind what is most beneficial for students. Grading fatigue can happen, too, when grading alone. The more time we spend looking at the same assignment, the less consistent our opinions become. The students at the top of the stack usually get the best of us, while those at the bottom could potentially get a cursory read.

Introduce the difference between reflection and self-evaluation to the students. As with the no-grades mindset, this will take a little convincing, but starting with a conversation about why students will be evaluating themselves helps to grease the wheel. Students also need to understand that while reflection is about the process of learning, the hows, whats and whys, the self-evaluation is the end result of that. Understanding the level of mastery achieved is the end result of the process demonstrated throughout the learning. Now the child must decide if he or she has met his or her goal.

Help students develop their own self-assessment tools. The key here is to do it with the kids and not alone. Single point rubrics work well. You can create one by making three columns on a piece of paper. Place the skills or content in the center and leave the columns on either side blank so students can fill them in to indicate their level of proficiency. On the right they will note areas of concern and on the left they will show areas that exceed standards. Students fill in evidence on either or both sides, based on the standard or skill. Or let kids group up to develop a rubric based on the standards the assignment asks them to address. Have them indicate proficiency by referring to specifics in the work they did.

A BLUEPRINT FOR FULL IMPLEMENTATION

Step 1: Discuss the new role students will play in the assessing process.

Students will need to have some kind of understanding of mastery learning when they have to grade themselves. Because you are no longer working with a point or letter scale, which is all they have known, you will need to provide them with something else to measure themselves by. You will need to help kids grasp mastery learning the same way you taught them about the no-grades mindset. Their understanding is key to their ability to assist in collaboration for their end "report card" if the school requires one. Essentially, they will be determining the grade with the teacher's support rather than the other way around.

Step 2: Provide a checklist to help scaffold the self-assessment process.

Students will need some guidance, especially at first, so either provide them with a basic checklist or generate one with their help to keep them focused while they assess. The checklist will need to include clear criteria that they are assessing themselves against. If they know what mastery looks like and in which areas they need to show it, that will streamline the process.

Step 3: Allow students to self-grade using evidence.

When students assess how they are doing, it's not good enough for them to say, "I deserve to be considered proficient because I know what I did." They need to be more specific, taking evidence from their work that supports their assessment. Often I tell students it's like writing an argument paper. You make an assertion about something and then you need to support the assertion with evidence from the text. In this analogy, the "text" is their assignment and this is where they draw their support from.

See below for an excerpt of exemplary student work. Anastasia Papatheodorou was a senior in my AP Literature and Composition class. She was one of my hardest sells about giving up grades and also one of my greatest success stories.

> For starters, I'll get straight to how I have done this term specifically. I most definitely had my lazy moments this term. Right when I was struck by the deadly senioritis, it came time for a fifteen-page research paper. That was definitely tough to get through, but I was pretty proud of myself after that. Although it

still needed more work, I think that paper definitely showed an improvement in development. As I mentioned in my last reflection, depth has been something I've struggled with all year, but I think this paper really showed how I started with an idea and I expanded on it. (Delineate and evaluate the argument and specific claims in a text, including the validity of the reasoning as well as the relevance and sufficiency of the evidence.)…

(specific evidence from her self-assessment was removed)

If I can take this class over I would want to continue to work on depth because I have improved, but just like with anything there is always room for improvement. I would want to focus on depth specifically because if there is any skill that will get you far in life it is being able to answer the question "Why?"

Well, it has come to that point that I dread so much talking about in conferences, which is why I chose to write about it instead. The grade I believe I deserve is an…wait for it…A. Not to say that I deserve an A just because, well who doesn't want an A, but I truly never worked so hard toward a class before to actually improve. I show clear growth in not just organization and cohesion but, thanks to you Ms. Sackstein, also public speaking, use of technology, researching, and most important, reflecting.

Step 4: Converse with students to determine a final grade if one is needed for the report card.

Once students have prepared to self-evaluate by going through their body of work, then it is time to discuss it with the teacher. The student should have gathered evidence and he or she should be certain of the evaluation. The teacher shouldn't drill the student, but rather listen attentively, asking clarifying questions to fill gaps. These conversations should take about five minutes. At the end, the student provides a grade that will go on the transcript or report card. Make sure to use the grade that is determined in the conversation; there should be no surprises.

If the teacher doesn't agree with the student, then a longer conversation needs to happen. It's important to talk it out. If in the end, the student really believes he or she deserves a particular grade, I'm inclined to say let him or her have it. After all, the grade itself doesn't mean very much. This happened a few times my first year, and it left me with an unpleasant feeling that I needed to address personally. Because of the traditional beliefs I held at that time, I felt uneasy allowing the student to have the grade. Despite this challenge, however, I did allow the student's grade to appear on the report card.

OVERCOMING PUSHBACK

People will say that teachers are the only ones qualified to assess or evaluate students, and therefore sharing this responsibility is lazy on behalf of teachers. I've already addressed how teachers are intimately involved with helping students to assess themselves, which sometimes is more work than simply giving a grade would be. It should be clear, too, how much students benefit from learning how to self-assess. This resistance seems to stem from another source of tension: How can we control the students if they have power over their own grades? Honestly, teachers and parents are the ones who need the grades. Grades are often used to motivate or punish, making them very powerful tools that both teachers and parents can use to get students to do things they may not want to do. This pushback isn't insurmountable.

All students would inflate or deflate their own grades. You'd think that, but most students are actually pretty honest, and those who aren't really just require a frank conversation. There is no shaming necessary—just ask a few questions and they will usually make the necessary adjustments. When students will not alter the grade (and they are very few), ask them to present their work and have them look at theirs next to an exemplar. Ask them to make comparisons. Ultimately the evaluation needs to come from them, so our job is to help them see what is in front of them objectively.

What about the student who does no work, but still thinks he or she should pass? Again, a frank conversation is in order here. Perhaps you talk to the student about what he or she knows. Believe it or not, just because work hasn't been completed, doesn't mean learning hasn't happened. We do need evidence of learning, but sometimes a conversation and alternative assignment can do the trick.

"But I don't want to give myself a grade." Some students may resist self-evaluation, and that is probably because they don't feel confident in what they see and feel about themselves. It is important to help students understand that they are the only ones who truly know what they know and understand. If they don't want to work alone to develop their evaluation, partner with them and help them build their confidence. You may hear things like, "I hate this part" or "I don't like grading myself." I usually answer with, "I don't like grading you either; that's why we're doing it like this. This grade isn't a measure of what you know and can do, it is just a formality."

How can I allow this student to get this grade? Okay, so here's a tricky one. You may find that you have some conflicting feelings about putting the control into the student's hands. I'd be lying if I said there weren't one or two conferences where I really didn't agree with what the students said, and despite my best effort to help them understand my view, they held their positions. I needed to take a breath and remember that the grade isn't important and if this was the level students really believed they had attained, I had to trust them as much as I trust the process. Be patient and try to move past the "justice" reflex. It's not about fairness; it's about mastery achievement.

> It's time to pass the baton to the students and watch in amazement as they skillfully share what they have learned.

THE HACK IN ACTION

Perhaps the greatest trepidation I had this year was placing the responsibility for final grading into my students' hands. Like most educators, I was used to handling the burden on my own (and I think I secretly liked to have the power), but grading had come to seem arbitrary and tiresome, and so when it came time to test the effectiveness of our changes in tracking achievement, it was only fitting that the students assumed control of their grades, just as they had managed other aspects of their assessments.

First, I sent out a survey to see how students would like to communicate their final grades. They could choose to share them in writing, on Voxer with an audio file, on video or screencast, or in a one-to-one conference. Once I got a preliminary idea of how many students were going to do what, it was time to provide some instruction about the expectations.

Preparing for final self-assessments - directions

It's the end of year and now it's time to really think about what you've learned. In preparation for your end of the year self-assessment, I'd like you to prepare a bunch of things…

Since there are several options for how you can present it (already signed up for) read the general information and then only the part that specifically refers to your delivery method.

General directions:

You will prepare your evidence of learning to show what you have mastered or at least become proficient in.

1. **Review the standards specific for your class**
2. **Review your work completed this year and the reflections**
3. **Determine which work shows your mastery against the standards**
4. **You should be able to show your learning in each of the core groups of learning with specific reference to the assignments:**

Reading	Speaking	Language
Writing	Listening	Technology

5. **Make sure to indicate your areas of growth**
6. **Did you meet your goals for the year?**
7. **What do you feel you could have done better? Why? How would you change this?**

If you are writing this out, make sure to comprehensively discuss the standards for each of the core areas and the assignments/projects that address each of the sections. Make sure to write it like a reflection with evidence from your work. Take screenshots to help show what you're talking about.

If you are using video, screencasting or speaking (Voxer or voice message), I recommend you plan what you're going to say first.

If you are having a conference with me, you must come prepared with above information and evidence. Think before you come.

The conference schedule will be given out over the next week for each class. Those of you doing an alternative form of reflection, your work is due on_____

Figure 9.1

The assignment sheet outlined specific deadlines so those students who were to meet with me face to face could prepare their evidence for the conference by the date we were scheduled to meet. My goal for having them prepare was to make sure students could show their mastery of the year-long standards by presenting evidence from their bodies of work. This avoids having any students arbitrarily inflate or deflate grades based on their feelings about learning in the class rather than their actual accomplishments. Whereas some students feel that they "deserve" a good grade regardless of their learning because they worked hard, some students believe that they "aren't good math students" or they are "humanities" people, and they downplay their achievements. Having them find specific evidence is a way of helping them be more objective and accurate.

As the written and video assignments began coming in, I realized quickly that I wasn't going to be disappointed with my choice to empower the students. Each display or written discussion of learning was cohesive, thoughtful, and evidence-based. Students had a candor in their writing and an honesty about growth and challenges that was most unexpected.

By the time I finished, I was completely impressed by how thorough students were. I had three students who believed they deserved to fail and gave me the reasons. Most students were spot on. Every child's assessment was what appeared on the report card. There were absolutely no surprises and no tears or angry emails on report card day.

Joy Kirr, a National Board Certified middle school English teacher, shared this example of how her seventh graders self-grade their reading.

> My students grade themselves on their independent reading. When the year begins, I ask each student to reflect on his or her reading habits each week. The first reflection sheet I give them asks them to evaluate six parts of their reading. Some students don't read an entire book, and most don't know how

many pages they've read, but it gets the conversation going. The first few reflections do not go into the grade book, as we're practicing how to reflect (and I really don't care for grades).

How did you do this week on your reading? Circle any that are true.

1. I read for an average of 20 minutes (or more) at home each day.
2. I remembered to bring my book home each day and back to school in the morning.
3. I got right into the reading zone whenever I was given free reading time at school.
4. I was always reading a book I enjoyed.
5. I finished _____ book(s) this week.
6. I read _____ pages this week.

This is the grade I deserve for reading this week _____ **out of 5 because** _____
_____
_____.

Figure 9.2

Still, some students are very hard on themselves. They'll give themselves a 9/10 because, "I finished it but not until the bus ride to school this morning" or "I really didn't try to understand parts that confused me." These make great discussion starters for one-on-one conferences. As the year moves forward, we continue with the reflection and new goal setting, whether it goes into the grade book or not. This reflection is the reason we are putting in all this time and effort; so students can see how they progress throughout the year.

It seems like no one enjoys grading, yet teachers are uncomfortable delegating the responsibility. We need to partner with our learners to create an environment where tracking progress and evaluating that process is transparent. It's time to pass the baton to the students and watch in amazement as they skillfully share what they have learned. Consider who does the grading now. How might you introduce self-evaluation into your practice? How might you model the activity for students? What impact would doing this kind of activity have on learning?

HACK 10

CLOUD-BASED ARCHIVES

Transition to portfolio assessment

There is incredible potential for digital technology in and beyond the classroom, but it is vital to rethink how learning is organised if we are to reap the rewards.
— GEOFF MULGAN, AUTHOR/PROFESSOR/STRATEGIST

THE PROBLEM: REPORT CARDS DON'T TELL THE WHOLE STORY

A REPORT CARD IS supposed to be a window into a student's learning; unfortunately, the light is usually out on the inside. The scores, which are often averaged, give a poor explanation of what students know and can do. In high school, teachers are often limited to one grade and pre-slugged comment codes for an entire term's learning. Much of the time the choices are inadequate to communicate student learning with any usefulness.

- Progress reports and report cards are too infrequent to show growth.

- Symbols don't give an accurate picture of learning.

- The comment space is restrictive.

- Students have little investment beyond what they "got."

- The report card isn't a tool for growth.

THE HACK: DEMONSTRATE LEARNING WITH DIGITAL PORTFOLIOS

Digital portfolios provide a place for students to demonstrate growth using real evidence of learning. With each artifact they collect, students have the opportunity to reflect on the work and add nuance to their self-assessments. Because students select their own artifacts, digital portfolios become living files of progress over the course of students' academic lives, and learning doesn't have to end with each school year.

Imagine having access to the digital portfolio of incoming students in addition to state test scores. You could see what students know and can do, where they ended the previous year, and where they need improvement. Digital portfolios create a virtual time capsule for high school students, illustrating growth over many school years. When entering college, students can show admissions officers real work—examples of performance and progress that say much more about learning than a GPA ever could.

WHAT YOU CAN DO TOMORROW

Since students should be in charge of their portfolios, make it possible for them to maintain paper or digital folders in the classroom so they can start gathering evidence of their learning right away.

Determine the best tool for artifact collection. There are many different ways to do this. Some programs, like Richer Picture or FreshGrade, offer various plans, including site licenses that school districts can purchase. Google and Microsoft provide alternatives from familiar names. Other Learning Management Systems, like Edmodo and Schoology, have their own modules for collecting digital data. Teacher comfort is important; it's a matter of finding a tool that will easily collect and transfer student artifacts each year. Try one tool tomorrow and another the day after. Soon, you'll know what works best for you and your students.

Distinguish between portfolios and report cards. Prepare a mini-lesson that helps students understand why portfolios are a better representation of their learning and the true purpose of moving away from the traditional report card. Help students understand the power of sharing their best work in contrast with the grade on a report card given by a teacher. Lead brainstorming sessions about how to create digital portfolios that best represent achievement and are easily accessible to a wide audience.

Review reflection practices. All selected work should include a reflection. Make sure that students understand that every piece of selected work will require a reflection that tells why it was selected and what learning it exhibits. Learners should also be able to express what they learned rather than just pointing out feedback that the teacher or a peer provided. Review Hack 8 for specifics and guiding questions for reflections.

A BLUEPRINT FOR FULL IMPLEMENTATION

Step 1: Work with students to determine criteria for artifact selection.

Consider what it is that students are trying to show in their portfolios: Is it going to be growth in specific areas? Mastery? Connection?

As a class, determine what portfolios should present, and then help students review all of their work to determine which products meet the criteria. Remember that the decision to include something must always be the student's if the process is to remain authentic.

Over the course of the year, you may require students to collect specific assignments because they fit criteria, but collecting a piece doesn't mean it must end up in the finished portfolio. One of the greatest skills students learn in this process is how to select the best examples and express why they have been added.

Step 2: Teach students to connect learning across content areas and time.

Although we love to see students connect learning within a discipline, it is much better when they can connect skills and content across subjects. A testament to mastery is the ability to use skills independently in different areas. While students are selecting pieces for their portfolios, it should be evident in their reflections and choices that they see both obvious and subtle connections to other subject areas.

Step 3: Plan class time for portfolio work.

We must give class time to what we value: If we are going to tell students this is an important activity, we can't assign it and expect them to do it on their own. Make time for students to work independently, with classmates, and with the teacher to ensure a more successful experience. This will also provide opportunities for students to practice different ways to collect artifacts—pictures, podcasts, videos, blog posts, etc. Plus, class time gives the teacher the chance to observe this important process of creating, collecting, and reflecting on artifacts that demonstrate learning.

Step 4: Present final portfolios to hone reflection and speaking skills.

Often when students complete an assignment, only the teacher, and possibly their parents, view it. By requiring students to present portfolios to the class, to a committee of some kind, or to visiting educators, students will extend the learning experience by considering how to narrow their focus and appeal to an audience in the presentation. Plus, this is yet another opportunity to practice reflection on learning.

It's helpful to have a question-and-answer period at the end of each presentation so students address any areas of confusion and dig deeper into their own understanding of their learning. Answering a question may elicit connections that aren't evident in their presentations.

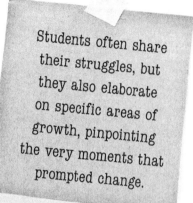

Students often share their struggles, but they also elaborate on specific areas of growth, pinpointing the very moments that prompted change.

To extend the audience for the presentations, use apps like Periscope to live-stream them, or record them for future viewing. Exceptional presentations can be included in an exemplar database, which will help future students learn how to efficiently present their own learning.

OVERCOMING PUSHBACK

Some people might suggest that portfolios do not represent all of a student's learning and are not an appropriate evaluation instrument. They are conditioned to equate achievement to a grade, so they will push back. Here are a few examples of this pushback and how you can react.

What's the point of doing portfolio conferences if I talk to my child every day? At portfolio conferences, students discuss their learning by referring to actual artifacts. Talking to your child daily about learning is awesome, but when you take the time to go to school, or to review a digital portfolio, you become part of the learning experience. This goes beyond casual chats about school at home; your child sees your commitment to the learning process and your support of the teacher's strategy.

Portfolios aren't a replacement for report cards. Some people will not see the value in collecting and talking about work in this manner. However, students become better, more metacognitive learners when they go through this process, and evidence of their learning will be obvious as they talk about their growth. Ask a child about a test score. Ask what he learned, what he remembers, or even why the score is a 70 or a 90. He may remember the grade but rarely can he explain the reason for it. Conversely, portfolios help students speak for themselves.

THE HACK IN ACTION

At the end of each school year, students at World Journalism Preparatory School (WJPS) are expected to give an exhibition of their learning. They review their portfolios for that year or multiple years and create a presentation that shows growth across content areas and the development of important life skills.

When they enter senior year, students understand that before graduation they need to speak about what they have achieved to a panel of listeners comprised of their peers, teachers, and administrators. These exhibitions give the speakers an opportunity to share evidence of their work, connect their learning across content areas, and discuss how they've overcome challenges throughout the year. At best, they present a well-balanced portfolio that displays a keen understanding of standards and growth. At worst, students speak with little evidence but can still articulate the takeaways.

For years now, I've been helping students prepare for these presentations. I've had the honor of listening to them share their journeys and have witnessed their willingness to answer questions about what they will take with them into the future. The finest of these portfolios are punctuated by a student's keen ability to articulate specific skills and strategies for personal development. Students often share their struggles, but they also elaborate on specific areas of growth, pinpointing the very moments that prompted change.

It would be the rare student who has taken out a progress report or report card and tried to use it as a tool to show growth. At most, they look at the numbers or letters and view the trend of progress from one class to the next, not really considering what it all means. Most students understand how little these documents actually convey. The more important knowledge is what they were able to retain during classes and apply to future learning, and they share this during these powerful presentations of digital portfolios.

Can you imagine a world without report cards and transcripts? I can, and I'm hoping it happens soon. Portfolios offer an opportunity for students to show their learning and progress over time in a more comprehensive and meaningful way. Consider how portfolios might look in your classes. What would an end-of-year portfolio presentation look like in your class? Who could be on the audience panel? How might this experience round off a year more effectively than reviewing a simple report card? How do digital portfolios impact the future of assessment?

CONCLUSION

HACK YOUR GROWTH

G RADING PRACTICES HAVE been ingrained in us for as long as the educational system has existed, but society has changed; we are no longer training students for success in the industrial era. In the 21st century, we nurture critical thinkers and collaborators, innovators and problem solvers; we must if we want our world to thrive. The way we assess our students affects their perception of learning, so if we take the negative or superficially positive away from the experience, more students will be able to see the brilliance that lies beneath the number and letter grades.

What can you change about your assessment practices tomorrow? What will you change in the future?

I remember when I decided it was time to throw out grades. It occurred to me that I would be surrounded by others who didn't agree with my philosophy. Regardless of the realization that I might be on a solo journey, I took the leap. Not knowing exactly how I would make it a reality or what kind of pushback I would receive, I was undeterred from moving forward.

Now a few years into this process, still working in a school that doesn't ascribe to this belief system, I struggle. Each year, I must hit the reset button with new students, engage in the tough conversations, challenge their attitudes about learning and continue to stand firm in my understanding of how assessment without grades will benefit my students. They often resist what they don't understand. I've had students share their fears with me about the changes in assessment and their worries about how the colleges they apply to won't understand. I listen patiently, quelling their apprehension, assuring them that what we're doing will improve their ability to grow as learners and human beings.

They don't always trust me at first. I feel their skepticism, understanding that eventually they will suspend that fear and put their faith in me. It's a tremendous responsibility that I take very seriously. Fortunately, I know what they cannot understand yet, that once they are freed from the confining nature of the grading system, they will truly flourish.

We don't do what we do for the thanks or for the opportunity to say, "I told you so," but there is a deep satisfaction in the commitment we make to our students and their growth as people. Taking this leap has profoundly changed my practice and the opportunities allotted to my students. When a student asks without me offering, "Can I redo this?" and not because they want a better grade, but because they truly want to develop mastery of the content, I know the no-grades classroom works. Students inherently want to grow and learn; their curiosity drives them in ways that are hard to explain. The traditional system deprives them of that curiosity and once detached from it, they forget the spark. By hacking assessment and building an ongoing conversation about learning, we empower them to reignite it.

As you embark on this journey, you will have the support, as I did, of folks from your Personal Learning Network, people who get it and although they may not be in your school, they are just a tweet away. You may have days when you feel down and want to revert back because it's easier than pushing forward, but you will gain solace in knowing that you are changing the way students think about learning.

Making these changes transformed learning in my classroom in ways I couldn't have imagined. I suspected it might, but really had no evidence until it was implemented for a full year and my students told me they got it. Through emails and conversations with students, I've learned the power of the shift away from grades, and it has solidified my resolve and helped me to push on.

If you're ready to see your students thrive and to bring joy and curiosity back to your classroom, take a risk: Make the change to a no-grades classroom and watch it happen. The work will be worth it.

OTHER BOOKS IN THE
HACK LEARNING SERIES

HACKING EDUCATION
10 Quick Fixes For Every School

By Mark Barnes (@markbarnes19) & Jennifer Gonzalez (@cultofpedagogy)

In the bestselling *Hacking Education*, Mark Barnes and Jennifer Gonzalez employ decades of teaching experience and hundreds of discussions with education thought leaders to show you how to find and hone the quick fixes that every school and classroom need. Using a hacker's mentality, they provide **one Aha moment after another** with 10 Quick Fixes For Every School—solutions to everyday problems and teaching methods that any teacher or administrator can implement immediately.

"Barnes and Gonzalez don't just solve problems; they turn teachers into hackers—a transformation that is right on time."

— DON WETTRICK, AUTHOR OF *PURE GENIUS*

MAKE WRITING
5 Teaching Strategies That Turn Writer's Workshop Into a Maker Space
By Angela Stockman (@angelastockman)

Everyone's favorite education blogger and writing coach, Angela Stockman, turns teaching strategies and practices upside down in the bestselling, *Make Writing*. She spills you out of your chair, shreds your lined paper, and launches you and your writer's workshop into the maker space! Stockman provides five right-now writing strategies that reinvent instruction and **inspire both young and adult writers** to express ideas with tools that have rarely, if ever, been considered. *Make Writing* is a fast-paced journey inside Stockman's Western New York Young Writer's Studio, alongside the students there who learn how to write and how to make, employing Stockman's unique teaching methods.

"Offering suggestions for using new materials in old ways, thoughtful questions, and specific tips for tinkering and finding new audiences, this refreshing book is inspiring and practical in equal measure."

— **AMY LUDWIG VANDERWATER,** AUTHOR AND TEACHER

HACKING THE COMMON CORE
10 Strategies for Amazing Learning in a Standardized World
By Michael Fisher (@fisher1000)

In *Hacking the Common Core,* longtime teacher and CCSS specialist Mike Fisher shows you how to bring fun back to learning, with 10 amazing hacks for teaching all Core subjects, while engaging students and making learning fun. Fisher's experience and insights help teachers and parents better understand close reading, balancing fiction and nonfiction, using projects with the Core, and much more. *Hacking the Common Core* provides **read-tonight-implement-tomorrow strategies** for teaching the standards in fun and engaging ways, improving teaching and learning for students, parents, and educators.

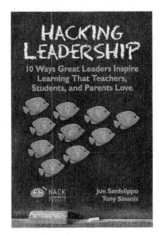

HACKING LEADERSHIP
10 Ways Great Leaders Inspire Learning That Teachers, Students, and Parents Love

By Joe Sanfelippo (@joesanfelippoFC) and Tony Sinanis (@tonysinanis)

In the runaway bestseller *Hacking Leadership*, renowned school leaders Joe Sanfelippo and Tony Sinanis bring readers inside schools that few stakeholders have ever seen – places where students not only come first but have a unique voice in teaching and learning. Sanfelippo and Sinanis ignore the bureaucracy that stifles many leaders, focusing instead on building a culture of **engagement, transparency, and most important, fun.** *Hacking Leadership* has superintendents, principals, and teacher leaders around the world employing strategies they never before believed possible.

"The authors do a beautiful job of helping leaders focus inward, instead of outward. This is an essential read for leaders who are, or want to lead, learner-centered schools."

— GEORGE COUROS, AUTHOR OF THE INNOVATOR'S MINDSET

HACKING LITERACY
5 Ways To Turn Any Classroom Into a Culture Of Readers
By Gerard Dawson (@gerarddawson3)

In *Hacking Literacy*, classroom teacher, author, and reading consultant Gerard Dawson reveals 5 simple ways any educator or parent can turn even the most reluctant reader into a thriving, enthusiastic lover of books. Dawson cuts through outdated pedagogy and standardization, turning reading theory into practice, sharing **valuable reading strategies**, and providing what *Hack Learning Series* readers have come to expect – actionable, do-it-tomorrow strategies that can be built into long-term solutions.

HACKING ENGAGEMENT
50 Tips & Tools to Engage Teachers and Learners Daily

By James Alan Sturtevant (@jamessturtevant)

Some students hate your class. Others are just bored. Many are too nice, or too afraid, to say anything about it. Don't let it bother you; it happens to the best of us. But now, it's **time to engage!** In *Hacking Engagement*, the seventh book in the *Hack Learning Series*, veteran high school teacher, author, and popular podcaster James Sturtevant provides 50 – that's right five-oh – tips and tools that will engage even the most reluctant learners daily.

HACKING HOMEWORK
10 Strategies That Inspire Learning Outside the Classroom
By Starr Sackstein (@mssackstein) and Connie Hamilton (@conniehamilton)

Learning outside the classroom is being reimagined, and student engagement is better than ever. World-renowned author/educator Starr Sackstein has changed how teachers around the world look at traditional grades. Now she's teaming with veteran educator, curriculum director, and national presenter Connie Hamilton to bring you **10 powerful strategies** for teachers and parents that promise to inspire independent learning at home, without punishments or low grades.

"Starr Sackstein and Connie Hamilton have assembled a book full of great answers to the question, 'How can we make homework engaging and meaningful?'"

— **Doug Fisher and Nancy Frey,** Authors and Presenters

HACKING PROJECT BASED LEARNING
10 Easy Steps to PBL and Inquiry in the Classroom

By Ross Cooper (@rosscoops31) and Erin Murphy (@murphysmusings5)

As questions and mysteries around PBL and inquiry continue to swirl, experienced classroom teachers and school administrators Ross Cooper and Erin Murphy have written a book that will empower those intimidated by PBL to cry, "I can do this!" while at the same time providing added value for those who are already familiar with the process. *Hacking Project Based Learning* demystifies what PBL is all about with **10 hacks that construct a simple path** that educators and students can easily follow to achieve success.

"*Hacking Project Based Learning* is a classroom essential. Its ten simple 'hacks' will guide you through the process of setting up a learning environment in which students will thrive from start to finish."

— **DANIEL H. PINK,** *NEW YORK TIMES* BESTSELLING AUTHOR OF *DRIVE*

HACK LEARNING ANTHOLOGY
Innovative Solutions for Teachers and Leaders
Edited by Mark Barnes (@markbarnes19)

Anthology brings you the most innovative education Hacks from the first nine books in the *Hack Learning Series*. Written by twelve award-winning classroom teachers, principals, superintendents, college instructors, and international presenters, *Anthology* is every educator's new problem-solving handbook. It is both a preview of nine other books and a **full-fledged, feature-length blueprint** for solving your biggest school and classroom problems.

HACKING GOOGLE FOR EDUCATION
99 Ways to Leverage Google Tools in Classrooms, Schools, and Districts

By Brad Currie (@bradmcurrie), Billy Krakower (@wkrakower), and Scott Rocco (@ScottRRocco)

If you could do more with Google than search, what would it be? Would you use Google Hangouts to connect students to cultures around the world? Would you finally achieve a paperless workflow with Classroom? Would you inform and engage stakeholders district-wide through Blogger? Now, you can say Yes to all of these, because Currie, Krakower, and Rocco remove the limits in Hacking Google for Education, giving you **99 Hacks in 33 chapters**, covering Google in a unique way that benefits all stakeholders.

"Connected educators have long sought a comprehensive resource for implementing blended learning with G Suite. *Hacking Google for Education* superbly delivers with a plethora of classroom-ready solutions and linked exemplars."

— **Dr. Robert R. Zywicki,** Superintendent of Weehawken Township School District

HACKING ENGAGEMENT AGAIN
50 Teacher Tools That Will Make Students Love Your Class
By James Alan Sturtevant (@jamessturtevant)

50 Student Engagement Hacks just weren't enough. James Alan Sturtevant, a 33-year veteran classroom teacher, wowed teachers with the original *Hacking Engagement*, which contained 50 Tips and Tools to Engage Teachers and Learners Daily. Those educators and students got better, but they craved more. So, longtime educator and wildly popular student engager Sturtevant is *Hacking Engagement Again*!

"This book is packed with ideas that can be implemented right away: Some creatively weave technology into instruction, others are just plain creative, and all of them are smart. Plus, the QR codes take the reader to so many more fantastic resources. With this book in hand, every teacher will find ways to freshen up their teaching and make it fun again!"

— **JENNIFER GONZALEZ,** BESTSELLING AUTHOR, SPEAKER, AND CEO
AT CULTOFPEDAGOGY.COM

HACKING DIGITAL LEARNING STRATEGIES
10 Ways to Launch EdTech Missions in Your Classroom

By Shelly Sanchez Terrell (@ShellTerrell)

In *Hacking Digital Learning Strategies*, Shelly Sanchez Terrell, international EdTech presenter and NAPW Woman of the Year, demonstrates the power of EdTech Missions—lessons and projects that inspire learners to use web tools and social media to innovate, research, collaborate, problem-solve, campaign, crowdfund, crowdsource, and publish. The 10 Missions in *Hacking DLS* are more than enough to transform how teachers integrate technology, but there's also much more here. Included in the book is a **38-page Mission Toolkit**, complete with reproducible mission cards, badges, polls, and other handouts that you can copy and distribute to students immediately.

"The secret to Shelly's success as an education collaborator on a global scale is that she shares information most revered by all educators, information that is original, relevant, vetted, and proven, combining technology with proven education methodology in the classroom. This book provides relevance to a 21st century educator."

— THOMAS WHITBY, AUTHOR, PODCASTER, BLOGGER, CONSULTANT, CO-FOUNDER OF #EDCHAT

HACKING PARENTHOOD
10 Mantras You Can Use Daily to Reduce the Stress of Parenting
By Kimberley Moran (@kimberleygmoran)

You throw out consequences willy nilly. You're tired of solutions that are all or nothing. You're frustrated with the daily chaos. Enter mantras, invaluable parenting anchors wrapped in tidy packages. These will become your go-to tools to calm your mind, focus your parenting, and concentrate on what you want for your kids. Kimberley Moran is a parent and a teacher who works tirelessly to find best practices for simplifying parenting and maximizing parent-child communication. Using **10 Parent Mantras as cues to stop time and reset**, Moran shares concrete ways to parent with intention and purpose, without losing your cool.

HACKING CLASSROOM MANAGEMENT
10 Ideas To Help You Become the Type of Teacher They Make Movies About

By Mike Roberts (@BaldRoberts)

We've all seen the movies. A teacher faces a lackluster educational environment or encounters a classroom full of downtrodden students. Not only do movie teachers solve those problems, they make a profound impact in the process. Many educators set out to be that kind of teacher, and then reality gets in the way. The success or failure of a class hinges on effective classroom management. Modeling concepts through both real-world scenarios and via some of the best educators in cinema, Mike Roberts, the 2014 Utah English Teacher of the Year, proves that learning to manage a classroom like a movie teacher is easier than you think. The best part is you can nail the role with just a few simple tweaks to what you're already doing. The book's **10 classroom management hacks** will guide you there. To make things even easier, Roberts gives readers a peek "Behind the Scenes" of successful classroom management with a bonus activity, prompt, or template in each hack.

HACK LEARNING RESOURCES

All Things Hack Learning:

hacklearning.org

The Entire *Hack Learning Series* on Amazon:

hacklearningbooks.com

The Hack Learning Podcast, hosted by Mark Barnes:

hacklearningpodcast.com

Hack Learning on Twitter:

@HackMyLearning

#HackLearning

#HackingLeadership

#HackingLiteracy

#HackingEngagement

#HackingHomework

#HackingPBL

#MakeWriting

#HackGoogleEdu

#EdTechMissions

#ParentMantras

#MovieTeacher

Hack Learning on Facebook:

facebook.com/hacklearningseries

facebook.com/groups/hackingparenthood

Hack Learning on Instagram:

hackmylearning

The Hack Learning Academy:

hacklearningacademy.com

ABOUT THE AUTHOR

 **Starr Sackstein** is a National Board Certified teacher, popular author and speaker, and two-time Bammy Awards Finalist. She teaches English and journalism at World Journalism Preparatory School in Flushing, NY. She is a Dow Jones News Fund Special Recognition Adviser, *Education Update* Outstanding Educator, New York State Director of the Journalism Education Association and an internationally recognized leader in assessment strategies and the no-grades classroom movement.

Starr is the author of *Blogging for Educators* (Corwin, 2015), *Teaching Students to Self-Assess* (ASCD, 2015) and *The Power of Questioning* (Rowman and Littlefield, 2015). She also writes the "Work in Progress" blog for *Education Week Teacher* and co-moderates the often trending #sunchat on Twitter and the global Facebook group, Teachers Throwing Out Grades.

Balancing a busy teaching career with writing, speaking, blogging and being the mom to 10-year-old Logan is a challenging adventure. Seeing the world through his eyes reminds Starr why education needs to change for every child.

Talk to Starr Sackstein
mssackstein@gmail.com

@MsSackstein on Twitter

Starr Sackstein, MJE Facebook Fan page

PUBLICATIONS

Times 10 is helping all education stakeholders improve every aspect of teaching and learning. We are committed to solving big problems with simple ideas. We bring you content from experts, shared through multiple channels, including books, podcasts, and an array of social networks. Our mantra is simple: Read it today; fix it tomorrow. Stay in touch with us at HackLearning.org, at hashtag #HackLearning on Twitter, and on the Hack Learning Facebook group.

Printed in Great Britain
by Amazon